Design and Development of a New Algorithm for Customer Churn Prediction through Class Imbalance

Dr.M. Rajeswari

Published by

Design and Development of a New Algorithm for Customer Churn Prediction through Class Imbalance

ISBN 978-93-86638-83-0

Author

Dr.M. Rajeswari

Bonfring

309, 2nd Floor, 5th Street Extension, Gandhipuram,

Coimbatore-641 012.

Tamilnadu, India.

E-mail: info@bonfring.org

Website: www.bonfring.org

Phone: 0422 4213231

Acknowledgement

I am thankful to **Dr. G. James Pitchai, Honourable Vice-Chancellor, Bharathiar University** for permitting me to carry out my research work. I thank **Dr.P.K. Manoharan, Respected Registrar, Bharathiar University** for providing permission to carry out my research work.

With pride and pleasure, I seize this opportunity to record my deep sense of gratitude to my guiding light **Dr. (Mrs.) T. DEVI, Professor and Head, Department of Computer Applications,** Bharathiar University, for her inspiring Guidance, meticulous planning, through comments, constructive criticism, persistent efforts and fruitful discussions. It is really my good fortune to do this research under her guidance, while she has certainly improved my academic personality.

I take this opportunity to express my gratitude to the **faculty members, research scholars and non-teaching staff members** of the **School of Computer Science and Engineering, Bharathiar University**, for their timely help.

I bestow my gratitude to my husband and my son who co-operated to the maximum extent during my research, I express my heartfelt thanks to my beloved father, mother without whose support achieving the success in the dissertation would be impossible.

The amount of encouragement received especially from my friends requires a special mention. I record my deep indebtedness to them for their support.

Dr.M. Rajeswari

Abbreviations

ANN	Artificial Neural Networks
ARPU	Average Revenue per User
ARUS	Advanced Random Under Sampling
AUC	Area Under Curve
CAD	Computer Assisted Design
CAM	Computer Aided Methods
CART	Classification and Regression Tree
CCP	Customer Churn Prediction
CLV	Customer Lifetime Value
CLV	Customer's Lifetime Value
CPM	Construction Project Management
CRM	Customer Relationship Management
CRT	Classification and Regression Tree
DL	Description Length
DM	Data Mining
DT	Decision Tree
DTR	Decision Tree Regression
EC	Evolutionary Computation
EMS	Evaluation Metrics
FL	Fuzzy Logic
GA	Genetic Algorithm
GB	Gradient Boosting
GP	Genetic Programming
IREP	Incremental Reduced Error Pruning
IT	Information Technology
KDD	Knowledge Discovery in Databases

KDP	Knowledge Discovery Process
k-NN	k-Nearest Neighbor
KPI	Key Performance Indicator
LOY	Customer Loyalty Index Scores
MA	Marketing Automation
MRA	Modified Ripper Algorithm
MRP	Modified Repeated Incremental Pruning to Produce Error Reduction
MTD	Mixture Transition Distribution
OSS	One-Sided Selection
PC	Probabilistic Computing
RA	Ripper Algorithm
RIPPER	Repeated Incremental Pruning to Produce Error Reduction
ROC	Receiver Operating Characteristic
ROS	Random Over Sampling
RQI	Relative Quality Importance
RUS	Random Under Sampling
SA	Service Automation
SAT	Satisfaction Index Scores
SFA	Sales-Force Automation
SVM	Support Vector Machines
WRF	Weighted Random Forest
YEAR	Year of Data

Summary

This research is concerned with the design and development of a new algorithm for predicting customer churn using class imbalance. Recent years are envisaging intense competition in banking sectors and as a consequence, the majority of banks are paying more attention on Customer Churn Prediction (CCP). CCP is considered as a major issue in Customer Relationship Management (CRM) and is one of the most important and helpful analysis task used by bankers to maintain credit card holders. Churning refers to the gross rate of customer loss during a given period and represents the loss of a customer. Banking sectors are increasingly acknowledging the need to change business strategies to focus on identifying customers most likely to churn and focus on techniques to minimize customer churn. This awareness is due to the fact that it is generally much more expensive to attract new customers than it is to retain and sell to existing ones. Churning is considered as a rare object and has great value and interest with bankers. Prediction, a sub-task of data mining, is a proven technique in various applications like fault diagnosis, anomaly detection, medical diagnosis, e-mail filtering, face recognition, oil spill and for predicting credit card holders churning behavior. A predictive model is defined as one that takes patterns that have been discovered in the database, to predict a future event. One major concern of CCP is that, the class distribution of customer data is often imbalanced, which degrades the performance of prediction. A class imbalance is a term where one class occurs much more often than the other. This study, to solve the problem of class imbalance during prediction for churn prevention, uses sampling methods and predictors to effectively predict and prevent churn with credit card holders.

Despite of this diversity, work related to handling of imbalanced data for churning is still sparse and most of the proposed algorithms and techniques degrade while handling churning with imbalance class. Sampling techniques like under-sampling and over-sampling are popular techniques applied for class-imbalance. Over-sampling method deals with imbalanced class problem and then used in Support Vector Machine (SVM) to predict customer churn. Advanced rule induction technique to build comprehensible churn prediction model that used over-sampling method to overcome the class imbalance among the training models. Recently, the application of condensed set based on co-operative co-evolution to handle imbalance datasets. Although, all these achievements have made a big contribution to customer churn prediction area, the work still is in search for models that can produce results with high accuracy and speed. The six categories of problems are associated while mining imbalanced classes. They are improper evaluation metrics, lack of data, relative lack of data, data fragmentation, inappropriate inductive bias and noise. To solve these issues, the present work considers, improper evaluation metrics, sampling, learn only the rare classes, non-greedy search techniques and more appropriate inductive bias.

Experiments were conducted to evaluate the performance of the proposed solutions to each data mining problem using a credit card holder dataset. The dataset consists of 1,00,000 records with 20 attributes. To compare classification algorithms, k-fold cross validation method was used to estimate the accuracy of the algorithms. Classification results of the three sampling methods such as Random Over Sampling (ROS), Random Under Sampling (RUS) and Advanced Random Sampling (ARUS) are used and algorithms such as Decision Tree Regression (DTR), Gradient Boosting (GB) and Weighted Random Forest (WRF), Genetic Algorithm (GA), k-Nearest Neighbor (k-NN), Ripper Algorithm (RA) and Modified Ripper Algorithm (MRA) are applied for solving the data mining problem related to customer churn prediction.

From the various results, it can be seen that the churn prediction process has been improved GA, k-NN, RA and the proposed algorithm MRA is successful. Careful analysis further revealed that under-sampling leads to improved prediction accuracy. AUC and CUBE do not show any increase in predictive performance when compared with other under-sampling methods. Weighted random forests, as a cost-sensitive learner, perform significantly better. However, the performance of the modified ripper algorithm was better when compared to all other solutions. The Modified Ripper Algorithm showed an efficiency gain when compared with the Ripper Algorithm while using the ROS, RUS, ARUS sampling methods respectively. To obtain an extra edge over competitive business, banking sectors are relying more and more on CRM combined with data mining techniques. In this study, churning behavior of credit card holders is predicted in the presence of class imbalance. Presence of imbalance during churn process reduces the efficiency of prediction and therefore has to be handled carefully. Five types of rare case categories were identified and nine types of predictors were proposed to handle class imbalance in credit card holder churning prediction.

Experimental results showed that all the methods (GA, k-NN, RA) used are successful for churn prediction in banking sector. However, the proposed new algorithm-Modified Ripper Algorithm outperforms all the other algorithms.

<table>
<tr><th>Chapter</th><th>Contents</th><th>Page No</th></tr>
</table>

CHAPTER 1

INTRODUCTION

1.1. Introduction

This research is concerned with the study and analysis of customer churn in order to improve the efficiency and effectiveness of customer churn prediction. It is becoming common knowledge in business that retaining existing customers is an important strategy to survive in industry. Once identified, these customers can be targeted with proactive retention campaigns in a bid to retain them. These proactive marketing campaigns usually involve the offering of incentives to attract the customer into carrying on their service with the supplier. These incentives can be costly, so offering them to customers who have no intention to defect results in lost revenue. Also many predictive techniques do not provide significant time to make customer contact. This time restriction does not allow sufficient time for capturing those customers who are intending to leave. This research aims to develop methodologies for predicting customer churn in advance, while keeping misclassification rates to a minimum.

1.2. Data Mining

In day to day life, the need of database and its use is getting increased and also it is never going to get decreased. The size of the database is also getting increased to the maximum, ranging from kilobyte, megabyte, gigabyte, terabyte, petabyte, exabyte, zettabyte, etc. Therefore it is in the special need of some technique which would fetch the data from the database, insert the data into the database and also manipulate it to produce the results. Data mining is the process of finding out the concealed predictive and descriptive information in such large databases. Data mining is a novel and dominant technology with a high possibility to help the companies note the high crucial information in the database which they have. Data mining sits on the universal subjects where subject includes database management, artificial intelligence, machine learning, and pattern recognition and data visualization.

Improvement of data acquisition and technology of storing a data given the result in the improvement of large sized huge databases. This showed the reflect in the area where human put high efforts starting from telephone call details, government statistics, credit card usage, transaction of data where to the toxic levels. Easy outlook of data mining is a necessary part in the discovery of knowledge in database.

The progression of discovery of knowledge involves the following steps (Omkar Singh Lodhi, 2012):

- Data Cleaning – deduction of Noisy data and inconsistent data.
- Data Integration – grouping of data from different sources.
- Data Selection – appropriate data is fetched from the database for the analysis.
- Data Transformation – Merging of data into a particular form which is like forming abstract of the data.
- Data Mining – Intellectual processes are used to bring out the outline of the data.
- Pattern Evaluation – Patterns are identified and evaluated.
- Knowledge Presentation–methods named visualization and knowledge representation are used to extract the mined knowledge to the end user.

Data preprocessing steps are 1 to 4. This step is used to for mining and as well for interacting the user and knowledge base. The appealing patterns are given to the user, where he/she may store it in a database which can be used for a future use. Data mining is a logical and investigative tool or a method which is designed to discover the data while searching the consistent patterns and/or systematic relationships between variables, and then to validate the new findings by applying the detected patterns to new subsets of data. The main objective of data mining is the prediction.

The most familiar type of data mining is predictive data mining which has the most wanted application in business field.

The data mining process involves the following stages:

- Exploration of initial data
- Building the model i.e., identification of pattern with verification and validation
- Exploitation of data (model which was built in the second stage is applied to data to create a prediction).

Data mining has been grown into an active and popular area of research due to its theoretical challenges and practical application domains associated with the problem of discovering interesting and previously unknown knowledge exist in the real-world databases. The major challenges to the data mining and the relevant contemplations in design and development of the algorithms are: Massive datasets and high dimensionality, over-fitting and assessing the statistical significance, understandability of patterns, non-standard incomplete data and data integration and mixed changing and redundant data.

1.2.1. *Tasks of Data Mining*

Data mining is used familiarly in the following specific set of six activities or tasks as listed below:

- Classification
- Estimation
- Prediction
- Affinity grouping or association rules
- Clustering
- Description and visualization

The first three tasks - classification, estimation and prediction are all examples of directed data mining or supervised learning. In directed data mining the most certain goal is to use the available data to build a model that describes one or more particular attribute(s) of interest (target attributes or class attributes) in terms of the rest of the available attributes. The following three tasks such as association rules, clustering and description are examples of undirected data mining such as no attribute is singled out as the target; the goal is to establish some relationship among all the attributes. Classification consists of examining the features of a newly presented object and assigning to it a predefined class. The classification task is characterized by the well-defined classes and a training set consisting of pre-classified examples. The task of classification is to build new models which are applied to unclassified data in order to classify it. Examples of classification tasks include: Classification of credit applicants as low, medium or high risk, Classification of mushrooms as edible or poisonous, Determination of which home telephone lines are used for internet access. Estimation deals with continuously valued outcomes. Given some input data the estimation to come up with a value for some unknown continuous variables such as income, height or credit card balance. Some examples of estimation tasks include: Estimating the number of children in a family from the input data of mothers education, Estimating total household income of a family from the data of vehicles in the family, Estimating the value of a piece of a real estate from the data on proximity of that land from a major business centre of the city.

Classification (or estimation) is used for modeling of any prediction and the difference are seems to be unapprised. Phone line can be classified using data mining. Data mining is used in internet access or a credit card transaction as fraudulent, the customer do not expect to be able to go back later to see if the classification was correct (Abdous et al., 2010). Sometimes classifications are correct and sometimes not correct. Imperfect knowledge only creates uncertainty in the real world. The appropriate steps include previously taken steps. The persons don't use the phone is primarily to dial the local Internet Service Provider (ISP) and occasionally only it takes place but with some efforts. Predictive tasks experiences are totally different because the records are classified according to expected future results or behavior. It is the only path to ensure the accuracy of the classification and to observe. Some examples of prediction tasks include: Predicting the size of the balance that will be transferred if a credit card prospect accepts a balance transfer offer, Predicting which customers will leave within next six months, Predicting which telephone subscribers will order a value-added service such as three-way calling or voice mail.

Classification and estimation techniques are used for prediction by utilizing training examples by which the value of the variable to be predicted is already known which contains chronological data for such examples. The chronological data is frequently taken in order to construct models which give explanation about the currently analyzed behavior. By applying this model to present inputs of the chosen research problem, the result is a prediction of future behavior with a maximum accurate value. Association rules involve relationship among the set of objects in a database is the association rule. In a specified set of transactions, each transaction are set of literals (called items), an association rule is denoted in the form of X Y, where X and Y are sets of items. The spontaneous meaning of that type of rule is that dealings of the database which contain X tend to contain Y. An example of an association rule is: '60'.'-12 of farmers that grow wheat also grow pulses; 2% of all farmers grow both of these items". Here 40% is called the confidence of the rule, and 2% the support of the rule. The solution is needed for the problem where the association rules that satisfy user-specified minimum support and minimum confidence constraints.

The process of segmenting diverse groups into a number of analogous subgroups or clump is called clustering. The main difference between clustering and classification is that clustering does not depend on predefined classes. Based on self clustering records are grouped together and it is often done as a preface to some other form of data mining or modeling. For example, in market cleavage attempt clustering might be the first step, rather than trying to coming with one size fits all models for determining whether the particular type works best for each cluster. Descriptive data mining's full strength depends in data visualization. It's always a tough task to come up with meaningful visualizations, but if it was found means then really it can be worth a thousand association rules since the human beings are tremendously practiced at extracting meaning from visual scenes. Planned systems describe knowledge discovery. The two types of goals are: (1) verification and (2) discovery. Through verification the systems are limited to verifying hypothesis of the user. Through discovery, the system finds new patterns automatically. The further division of discovery gives the prediction, where the system finds patterns for predicting the behavior of some entities and description about the future, also the system finds patterns for representation in human understandable form for the user.

1.2.2. *Techniques Used in Data Mining*

Every problem gives a way to derive useful knowledge from collection of data. Methods used for solving these problems are developed in the disciplines of statistics, machine learning and fuzzy sets. Also rough sets are directly pertinent to DM, in particular, to conceptual data exploration are used in pertaining each disciplines are introduced in this section. The difficulty of abstracting the information from data is undertaken by statisticians, lot of proposals was given for this research area but still it was lacking (Ferreira et al., 2004). Analysis of correlation is applies the numerical tools for analyzing the association between multiple variables. New method of discovering clusters in a very large set of objects described by vector of values is cluster analysis. To denote very important variables to describe cluster is factor analysis. Traditional methods which are used for classification of supervised tasks are Linear Discriminants, Quadratic k-Nearest Neighbor, Naive Bayes and Logistic Regression.

During the incorporation of subjects statistical methods face lot of difficulty; also there exist quantifiable information in their models. Assumption of various distributions of parameters and independence of attributes also considered. Conclusion of different studies concludes that machine learning will produce comparable predictive accuracy when comparing with the other. Machine learning performance is good as compared to statistical methods which can be attributed to the fact that it is free from the assumptions of parametric and structural's, which underlie in statistical methods (Collobert et al., 2002). The main disadvantage of statistical approaches to data analysis is problem of interpreting the results. Some of the machines learning techniques include:

- Neural Networks
- Genetic Algorithms
- Support Vector Machines
- Decision Tree Induction
- Fuzzy Logic

The computational models which are composed of numerous non linear processing elements are artificial neural networks which are arranged in a pattern similar to biological neuron networks. Usual neural network have activation value associated with every node and a value of weight which are associated with each connection. The governing of firing nodes is done by activation function and the propagation of data through network connections in massive parallelism. Training to the network can be given with examples through connection weight adjustments. Genetic algorithms are seeking/hunting algorithms established on mechanics of natural selection and natural genetics. The combination of endurance of the fittest among string structures with the randomized information exchange to form a search algorithm with some of the innovative flair of human search. Inside every new generation, a new set of strings will be used in the creation of bits and pieces of the fittest of the old (Ferreira et al.,2004). A rare new part is used for the measure of a good one. In the genetic algorithms which are randomized, have no simple random walk. Their efficient development historical information is needed to speculate on new search points with expected improved performance. A simple genetic algorithm which provides good result is composed of reproduction; crossover and mutation. Genetic algorithm gets differ totally from more normal optimization and search procedures in four ways: GA's work with coding of parameter se and not with the parameter themselves, search from a population of points, not a single point, use objective function information and not derivatives or other knowledge and user probabilistic transitional rules, not rules

The learning machines that perform the classification of binary and estimation of regression task are SVM. Due to important factors SVM is keep on increasing its popularity as a new paradigm of classification and learning because of two important factors. SVM minimize the expected error rather than the classification error and employ the duality theory of mathematical programming to get a dual problem that admits efficient computational methods. It is a new classification scheme which produces a tree and a set of rules, representing the model of different classes, from a given dataset. Fuzzy logic is out-looked as an expansion of classical logical systems which provides an effective conceptual framework for dealing with the problem of knowledge representation in an environment of uncertainty and imprecision. Some of the characteristics of fuzzy logic include: Exact reasoning is viewed as a limiting case of approximate reasoning, in fuzzy logic everything is a matter of degree, any logical system can be fuzzified and in fuzzy logic, knowledge is interpreted as a collection of elastic or equivalently, fuzzy constraint on a collection of variables.

1.2.3. Predictive Data Mining

Data mining is the development of exploration and analysis of data, by automatic or semi-automatic means, of large quantities of data in order to discover meaningful patterns and rules. Data mining can also be said or determined as the process of selecting, exploring and modeling large amounts of data to uncover previously unknown data patterns for business advantage. A large data sets can be classified is an important problem in data mining. The problem faced in classification can be denotes simply as follows, Database might have numerous number of records and classes, such that each record belongs to one of the given classes, the problem of classification is to decide the class to which a given record belongs. Still lots of problems are faced in simple classifying (Ling Xie et al., 2011). Descriptive models and predictive models are built using the data mining. The basic of unsupervised learning is descriptive models and the basic of supervised learning is predictive models (Janikow, 1993). One of the target variable or response variable is denotes as a function of other variable in the predictive mode. The problem faced in the prediction of churn is the response variable, i.e., status of the future denote that customers can take only two values which are Active and Churn. Predictive classification techniques are used in the churn modeling. Lot of predictive classification techniques is available which are namely Nearest Neighbor, Decision Tree, Linear Discriminant, Naive Bayes etc. In this research work, Decision Tree technique is used for prediction of churn (Ataee, 2005). The During the consideration specific requirements should be taken into account while designing any Decision Tree construction algorithms for data mining are that the method should be efficient in order to handle a very large sized databases and should be able to handle categorical attributes.

1.2.4. Data Mining vs Other Methods

Data mining vs. Statistics: The core of statistics is data mining only. The statistics helps to discriminate between random noise and significant findings, and also it provides a theory for approximating the probabilities of predictions, etc. Data Mining is further than Statistics. Data mining wrap the whole process of data analysis, which includes data cleaning, preparation, visualization of the results, how to generate predictions in real-time, etc. Statistics justifies the data in numbers and quantifies the data. There exist lot of tools for finding out the appropriate properties of the data but the statistics is very close pure mathematics. Data mining incorporates the use of statistics and other programming methods to discover patterns concealed in the data. Data mining builds a reaction about what the thing is really happening in some data. **Data mining vs. Machine Learning:** Data Mining normally goes only as far as interpreting the data, for example, categorizes newspaper articles based on their theme, or books according to the suitable age of readers). Data mining is a part of Machine Learning that is given raw data, then using Machine learning methods to extract some meaningful information about it (Mukherjea et al.,2005). The main aim of machine learning system is to determine the description of a given concept from a set of examples and from the background knowledge. Data mining aims to get succeed in large amount of data.

Data Mining vs. KDD: The steps involves in KDD (Knowledge Discovery in Databases) looks same as like the process of data mining, but it is not actually is. KDD is a division of computer science, which incorporates the tools and theories to help humans to mine the useful and previously unknown information from large collections of digitized data. (Fayyad et al., 1996, Chui at al., 2007). KDD have of many steps, where data mining is one of them. Data Mining is a use of an exact algorithm in order to extract patterns from data. **Data Mining vs. Predictive Analytics:** Predictive analytics is a part of statistical analysis which deals in extracting information from data and using it to predict about the future trends and behavior patterns. The heart of predictive analytics depends in capturing relationships between explanatory variables and the predicted variables from past occurrences, and to develop it to predict the outcomes of the future, where data mining has two major branches namely predictive and descriptive. **Data Mining vs. Business Intelligence:** Business intelligence is a sequence of information about a company's past performance which is used to predict the company's forthcoming performance. Data Mining allows the different users to filter huge amount of information available in data warehouses. It is from this sifting process that business intelligence gems may be found. Data mining is a technology and not a solution to the business; it is not a tool or framework.

1.3.   Customer Relationship Management

Customer Relationship Management (CRM) includes behavior and procedure planned to assist an organization to understand, communicate and service the needs of customers and prospects. The core of CRM is the fundamental philosophy, that is successful customer engagement, and successful business which is based on the ability to build significant relationships with customers. Different companies have their ideas in large quantity but with a meaningful relationship (Hoekstra and Huizingh, 1999, Ngai et al., 2009). For example Alice, don't know the names their millions of customers, but he have a very good idea of the preference across different market segmentations. They will hold the market through their mass media, and calculate consumer responses to different marketing operation.

CRM assist the business to understand who their customers are, the way to cooperate with the company, the rate of profit, and the value of their future. Also CRM assists the organization to make decisions in critical situations about how to do business, about as what will be their new products or services they should be developing in future, about the investment in the next season, etc. Efficient CRM gathers information about all the customers, analyze and interpret it. CRM is an information industry term for methodologies, software and usually Internet capabilities that help an enterprise manage customer relationships in an organized way

(Subhasish Das, 2007). CRM is the process of managing all aspects of interaction a company has with its customers, including prospecting, sales and service. CRM applications attempt to provide insight into and improve the company/customer relationship by combining all these views of customer interaction into one picture. CRM is an integrated approach to identifying, acquiring and retaining customers. By enabling organizations to manage and coordinate customer interactions across multiple channels, departments, lines of business and geographies, CRM helps organizations maximize the value of every customer interaction and drive superior corporate performance (Francis Buttle, 2008). CRM is an integrated information system that is used to plan, schedule and control the pre-sales and post-sales activities in an organization. CRM embraces all aspects of dealing with prospects and customers, including the call centre, sales-force, marketing, technical support and field service. The primary goal of CRM is to improve long-term growth and profitability through a better understanding of customer behavior. CRM aims to provide more effective feedback and improved integration to better gauge the return on investment (ROI) in these areas. CRM is a business strategy that maximizes profitability, revenue and customer satisfaction by organizing around customer segments, fostering behavior that satisfies customers and implementing customer centric processes.

There are four types of CRM which are Strategic CRM, Operational CRM, Analytical CRM, and Collaborative CRM (Subhasish Das, 2007). Strategic CRM is a heart of customer-centric business strategy which aims at winning and keeping profitable customers. Product-oriented strategic CRM: businesses believe that customers choose products with the best quality, performance, design or features, Production-oriented strategic CRM: businesses believe that customers choose low price products, Sales-oriented strategic CRM: businesses make the assumption that if they invest enough in advertising, selling, and public relations (PR) and sales promotion, customers will be persuaded to buy. Computerization of selling, marketing and service to the customer are focused by operational CRM. Marketing Automation (MA): It enforces the technologies to marketing processes to employ customer-related data in order to plan, develop, execute and evaluate targeted communications and offers, Sales-Force Automation (SFA): It enforces the technologies to the management of a company's selling activities. The method of selling the products can be decomposed into a number of stages, which are lead generation, lead qualification, needs identification, development of specifications, proposal generation, proposal presentation, handling objections and closing the sale, Service Automation (SA): It allows companies from large level to small level, manage their service operations, whether delivered through call centre, contact centre, web or face-to-face.

Analytical CRM aims in intelligent mining of customer-concerned data for strategic or tactical purposes. Analytical CRM focuses on enhancing value of a customer and company by capturing, storing, extracting, integrating, processing, interpreting, distributing, using and reporting customer-related data. Collaborative CRM applies technology across organizational boundaries with a view to optimizing company, partner and customer value. Collaborative CRM is the term used to describe the strategic and tactical alignment of normally separate enterprises in the supply chain for the more profitable identification, attraction, retention and development of customers. Banks deal with a large number of individual retail customers. Banks want CRM for its analytical capability to help them manage customer defection (churn) rates and to enhance cross-sell performance. Data mining techniques can be used to identify which customers are likely to defect, what can be done to win them back, which customers are hot prospects for cross-sell offers, and how best to communicate those offers. Banks want to win a greater share of customer spend (share of wallet) on financial services. In terms of operational CRM, many banks have been transferring service into contact centres and online in an effort to reduce costs, in the face of considerable resistance from some customer segments.

Churn Prediction

Churn is the gross rate of customer loss during a given period of time (that is, hourly or weekly or monthly or yearly). While formulating loss rate of customer, churn can be stated can be stated as follows.

$$Periodic\ Churn = \frac{C_0 + A_1 - C_1}{C_0}$$

Where:

C_0 : Number of customers at the beginning of the period.

C_1: Number of customers at the end of the period.

A_1: Gross new customers during the period.

The period of time depends on the organization that is the organization can give the period of time as hourly or weekly or monthly or yearly. The constant challenges on both sides of cost and revenue is customer churn, due to specific reasons the customer may move from one bank to another. The reasons may include the search of better trust worthiness, reliable products, plans and services. Inside the market the customer may find numerous choices because there are lots of competitions. By using the choices the user can choose the specific needed plan from the wide variety. The rates of churn are calculated with the increase in competition and deregulation. It is the loss, if the bank losses a single customer or more customer, where the loss of one bank become the profit of another bank. Augmented churn of customer will result in rising customer attainment costs and minimum average monthly transaction volumes (Hadden et al., 2006). Renewal of interest in bank is one of the things which make the customer satisfied and holding the bank for a long period of time. E- Banking needs more customers to retain an existing one where every customer need a new payment integrated infrastructure which in lies in between customer's company and banking corporation. It is the duty of the banks to identify the customers who generate low margins and put effort to develop strategies which increase margins or divest of such customers. It is always necessary to build, maintain and run sophisticated Customer Relationship Management (CRM) and Churn Management techniques in banks (Prasad and Madhavi, 2012). The important and universal business issue is the churn, where business sectors should efficiently manage to be viable, long-term market players.

Motivation

Churn prediction is the thrust research area in the field of CRM for past several decades. The focus on customer churn is to determinate the customers who are at risk of leaving and if possible on the analysis whether those customers are worth retaining. The churn analysis is highly dependent on the definition of the customer churn. The business sector and customer relationship affects the outcome how churning customers are detected. Example in credit card business customers can easily start using another credit card, so the only indicator for the previous card company is declining transactions. Hence this research focuses on churn prediction for banking sector.

1.4.   Objectives

In order to prevent customer churn, researchers have proposed a number of problems that arise when mining rare classes and rare cases. According to Weiss (2004), six categories of problems arise when mining imbalanced cases. The problems include improper evaluation metrics, lack of data, relative lack of data, data fragmentation, inappropriate inductive bias and noise. The main objective of the study is to investigate and analyse the techniques that can better handle class imbalance in churn prediction. The main objectives of this research are:

- To study in detail the data mining, customer relationship management, churn prediction and class imbalances.
- To analyze in detail the various techniques for handling class imbalance for predicting customer churn.
- To identify concepts to improve the effectiveness of handling class imbalance in churn prediction.

- To design and develop a prototype based on the above concepts.
- To test the prototype.

1.5.   Organization of the Thesis

This chapter provides introduction to data mining, problems in data mining, tasks performed in data mining, techniques and their comparison, a brief introduction to predictive data mining, CRM, churn prediction, motivation for this research work, problem statement and objectives.

Chapter 2 briefs on kinds of collection of information, need for data mining, the transformation of data into information, knowledge discovery in databases, various data mining models, data mining tasks, applications of data mining.

Chapter 3 discusses on customer relationship management, various dimensions on customer relationship management, literature review pertaining to classification frameworks in data mining models, churn prediction, traditional methods used in data mining for customer relationship management.

Chapter 4 discusses literature review on class imbalance, various research dimensions pertaining to class imbalance problem in churn prediction, various research methodologies used for class imbalance in churn prediction.

Chapter 5 deals with design and development of algorithm for identifying imbalance classes in customers churn at banking sector.

Chapter 6 discusses test on prototype based performance metrics, dataset taken and focuses on results and discussion on the algorithm along with the simulation tool.

Chapter 7 discusses the results obtained by testing the prototype with the test data.

Chapter 8 concludes the research, describes the contributions and limitations, and presents recommendations for further research.

CHAPTER 2

DATA MINING

2.1.　Introduction

As a result of constant increase of business needs, the amount of data in current database systems grows extremely fast. Since the cost of data storage keeps on dropping, users store all the information they need in databases. Moreover, people believe that by storing data in databases they may save some information that might turn up to be potentially useful in the future, in spite that it is not of direct value at the moment. Raw data stored in databases are seldom of direct use. In practical applications, data are usually presented to the users in a modified form, tailored to satisfy specific business needs. Even then, people must analyze data more or less manually, acting as sophisticated "query processors". This may be satisfactory if the total amount of data being analyzed is relatively small, but is unacceptable for large amounts of data. What is needed in such a case is an automation of data analysis tasks. That's exactly what KDD and DM provide. They help people improve efficiency of the data analysis they perform. They also make possible for people to become aware of some useful facts and relations that hold among the data they analyze and that could not be known otherwise, simply because of the overload caused by heaps of data. Once such facts and relations become known, people can greatly improve their business in terms of savings, efficiency, quality, and simplicity.

Typically, KDD/DM systems are not general-purpose software systems. They are rather developed for specific users to help them automate data analysis in precisely defined, specific application domains. Knowledge discovery is the process of nontrivial extraction of information from data, information that is implicitly present in that data, previously unknown and potentially useful for the user. The information must be in the form of patterns that are comprehensible to the user (such as, for example, If-Then rules). Knowledge is a pattern that is sufficiently interesting to the user and sufficiently certain. The user specifies the measure of interest and the certainty criterion. Discovered knowledge is the output from a program that analyzes a data set and generates patterns.

A pattern's certainty is the measure of confidence in discovered knowledge represented by the pattern. Discovered knowledge is seldom valid for all the data in the data set considered. Pattern's certainty is higher if data in the data set considered are good representatives of data in the database, if they contain little or no noise at all, if they are valid, reliable, complete, precise, and contain no contradictions.

Data mining is the process of pattern discovery in a data set from which noise has been previously eliminated and which has been transformed in such a way to enable the pattern discovery process. Data mining is always based on a data-mining algorithm. There must also be an application through which the user can select (from the database) and prepare a data set for KDD, adjust DM parameters, start and run the KDD process, and access and manipulate discovered patterns. KDD/DM systems usually let the user choose among several KDD methods. Each method enables preparation of a data set for automatic analysis, searching that set in order to discover/generate patterns (i.e., applying a certain kind of DM over that set), as well as pattern evaluation in terms of certainty and interest. KDD methods often make possible to use domain knowledge to guide and control the process and to help evaluate the patterns.

In such cases domain knowledge must be represented using an appropriate knowledge representation technique (such as rules, frames, decision trees, and the like). Discovered knowledge may be used directly for database query from the application, or it may be included into another knowledge-based program (e.g., an expert system in that domain), or the user may just save it in a desired form. Discovered patterns mostly represent some previously unknown facts from the domain knowledge. Hence they can be combined with previously existing and represented domain knowledge in order to better support subsequent runs of the KDD process. This chapter deals with data mining and various kinds of collection of information and the need for data mining. The method of transforming data into information, knowledge discovery in databases shortly termed as KDD, various data mining tasks are also presented. The data mining applications are discussed briefly in this chapter.

2.2. Data Mining

Data mining is not a new technology or advancement in computer science where the senses of the people are analyzed in the form of data on computers. Far past several decades, data mining has been referred as knowledge discovery, business intelligence, predictive modelling, predictive analytics, and so on. The definition of data mining may be defined as "Data mining is a business process for exploring large amounts of data to discover meaningful patterns and rules". The definition has several parts. Data mining is a business process which interacts with other business processes. Significantly, a process does not have a beginning and an end: it is ongoing. Data mining starts with data, then through analysis informs or inspires action, which, in turn, creates data that begets more data mining. The practical consequence is that organizations those want to outshine at using their data to improve their business do not view data mining as a sideshow. As a replacement for, their business strategy must include collecting data, analyzing data for long-term benefit, and acting on the results. At the same time, data mining readily fits in with other strategies for understanding market and customer. Market research, customer panels, and other techniques are compatible with data mining and more intensive data analysis (Da Ruan et al., 2005). The key is to recognize the focus on customers and the commonality of data across the enterprise.

A tool like Microsoft Excel is incredibly adaptable for working with relatively small amounts of data. Also, it allows a many varieties of computations on the values in each row or column; pivot tables are amazingly practical for understanding data and trends; and the charts offer a powerful mechanism for data visualization. Since computing power is readily available, a large amount of data is not a handicap, it is having more advantages. Data mining allows computers do what computers do best. It will dig through lots and lots of data which in turn provide people do what people do best, which is set up the problem and understand the results. The important part of the definition of data mining which has stated above is the part about meaningful patterns. Even though data mining can certainly be fun, helping the business is more important than amusing the miner. In many ways finding patterns in data is not tremendously hard. The operational side of the business generates the data, necessarily generating patterns at the same time. Yet, the goal of data mining is not to find just any patterns in data, but to find patterns that are useful for the business. Considering a call center application which assigns customers green colour denotes the meaning as very nice, since the caller is a valuable customer. The colour "yellow" refers to use some caution because the customer may be valuable but also has signs of some risk. The colour "red" denotes not to give the customer any special treatment because the customer is highly risky. Finding patterns can also mean targeting retention campaigns to customers who are most likely to leave. It can mean optimizing customer acquisition both for the short-term gains in customer numbers and for the medium- and long-term benefit in customer value (Cios et al., 2000, Jiawei Han et al., 2006).

Myriad data have been collected from simple numerical measurements and text documents, to more complex information such as spatial data, multimedia channels, and hypertext documents (David Hand et al., 2001). Here is a non-exclusive list of a variety of information collected in digital form in databases and in flat files. Every transaction in the business industry is infinity. Such transactions are usually time related and can be inter-business deals such as purchases, exchanges, banking, stock, etc., or intra-business operations such as management of in-house wares and assets. Large department stores, for example, the widespread use of bar codes, store millions of transactions daily representing often terabytes of data. Storage space is not the major problem, as the price of hard disks is continuously dropping, but the effective use of the data in a reasonable time frame for competitive decision-making is definitely the most important problem to solve for businesses that struggle to survive in a highly competitive world. In a Swiss nuclear accelerator laboratory counting particles, in the Canadian forest studying readings from a grizzly bear radio collar, on a South Pole iceberg gathering data about oceanic activity, or in an American university investigating human psychology, our society is having colossal amounts of scientific data that need to be analyzed.

From government census to personnel and customer files, very large collections of information are continuously gathered about individuals and groups. Governments, companies and organizations such as hospitals, are stockpiling very important quantities of personal data to help them manage human resources, better understand a market, or simply assist customers (Jiawei Han et al., 2006). Regardless of the privacy issues this type of data often reveals, this information is collected, used and even shared. With the amazing collapse of video camera prices, video cameras are becoming ubiquitous. Video tapes from surveillance cameras are usually recycled and thus the content is lost. However, there is a tendency today to store the tapes and even digitize them for future use and analysis. There is countless number of satellites around the globe: some are geostationary above a region, and some are orbiting around the Earth, but all are sending a non-stop stream of data to the surface. NASA, which controls a large number of satellites, receives more data every second than what all NASA researchers and engineers can cope with (David Hand et al., 2001). Many satellite pictures and data are made public as soon as they are received in the hopes that other researchers can analyze them.

The current society is collecting a tremendous amount of data and statistics about games, players and athletes. From hockey scores, basketball passes and car-racing lapses, to swimming times, boxer's pushes and chess positions, and all the data are stored. Commentators and journalists are using this information for reporting, but trainers and athletes would want to exploit this data to improve performance and better understand opponents. The explosion of cheap scanners, desktop video cameras and digital cameras is one of the causes of the outburst in digital media repositories. Also, many radio stations, television channels and film studios are digitizing their audio and video collections to improve the management of their multimedia assets. There are a multitude of Computer Assisted Design (CAD) systems for architects to design buildings or engineers to conceive system components or circuits. These systems are generating a tremendous amount of data. Moreover, software engineering is a source of considerable similar data with code, function libraries, objects, etc., which need powerful tools for management and maintenance. There are many applications making use of three-dimensional virtual spaces. These spaces and the objects they contain are described with special languages such as VRML. Ideally, these virtual spaces are described in such a way that they can share objects and places. There is a remarkable amount of virtual reality object and space repositories available. Management of these repositories as well as content-based search and retrieval from these repositories are still research issues, while the size of the collections continues to grow.

Most of the communications within and between companies or research organizations or even private people, are based on reports and memos in textual forms often exchanged by e-mail. These messages are regularly stored in digital form for future use and reference creating formidable digital libraries. Since the inception of the World Wide Web in 1993, documents of all sorts of formats, content and description have been collected and inter-connected with hyperlinks making it the largest repository of data ever built. Despite its dynamic and unstructured nature, its heterogeneous characteristic, and it's very often redundancy and inconsistency, the World Wide Web is the most important data collection regularly used for reference because of the broad variety of topics covered and the infinite contributions of resources and publishers. Many believe that the World Wide Web will become the compilation of human knowledge. Most data mining techniques have existed, at least as academic algorithms, for decades (Da Ruan et. al 2005). Data mining has become on a broad way due to the convergence of the following factors. The blend of these factors means that data mining is increasingly appearing as a foundation of business strategies. Data mining makes the most sense where large volumes of data are available. In fact, most data mining algorithms require somewhat large amounts of data to build and train models. The Web is not the only producer of voluminous data. Telephone companies and credit card companies were the first to work with terabyte-sized databases, an exotically large size for a database as recently as the late 1990s. That time has passed. Not only is a large amount of data being produced, but also, more and more often, it is being extracted from the operational billing, reservations, claims processing, and order entry systems where it is generated and then fed into a data warehouse to become part of the corporate memory. Data warehousing brings together data from many different sources in a common format with consistent definitions for keys and fields. Operational systems are designed to deliver results quickly to the end user, who may be a customer at a website or an employee doing the job. These systems are designed for the task at hand, and not for the task of maintaining clean, consistent data for analysis. The data warehouse, on the other hand, expected to be designed exclusively for decision support, which can simplify the job of the data miner.

Data mining algorithms typically require multiple passes over huge quantities of data. Many algorithms are also computationally intensive. The continuing dramatic decrease in prices for disk, memory, processing power, and network bandwidth has brought once-costly techniques that were used only in a few government-funded laboratories into the reach of ordinary businesses. Interest in Customer Relationship Management is Strong Across a wide spectrum of industries, companies have come to realize that their customers are central to their business and that customer information is one of their key assets. There exists a huge interval between the time when new algorithms first appear in academic journals and excite discussion at conferences and the time when commercial software incorporating those algorithms becomes available. There is another lag between the initial availability of the first products and the time that they achieve wide acceptance. For data mining, the period of widespread availability and acceptance has arrived. In recent years, new techniques are being developed however, much work is also devoted to extending and improving existing techniques.

A good data miner needs to have skills with numbers and a basic familiarity with statistics. Having a good working knowledge of Excel is also very useful, because it is the predominant spreadsheet in the business world. Spreadsheets such as Excel are very useful for analyzing smallish amounts of data and for presenting the results to a wide audience. Technical details are the demystification of data mining techniques. Although many are quite sophisticated, they are often based on a very accessible foundation. Another very important skill for a data miner is really an attitude. Lack of fear of large amounts of data and the complex processing that might be needed to squeeze out results. Working with large data sets, data warehouses, and analytic sandboxes is a key to successful data mining (Ian H. Witten et al., 2005).

At length, data mining is not just about producing technical results. No data mining model, for instance, ever really did anything more than shift bits around inside a computer. The results have to be used to help people in order to make more informed decisions. Producing the technical results is the end of the beginning of the data mining process. Being able to work with other people, communicate results, and recognize what is really needed are critical skills for a good data miner. Data is at the heart of many core business processes. It is generated by transactions in operational systems regardless of industry-retail, telecommunications, manufacturing, health care, utilities, transportation, insurance, credit cards, and financial services, for example. The promise of data mining is to find the interesting patterns lurking in all these billions and trillions of bits lying on disk or in computer memory (David Hand. et al,

2001). Data mining needs to become an essential business process, incorporated into other processes including marketing, sales, customer support, product design, and inventory control. Avoiding analytic effort starts with a willingness to act on the results. Many normal business processes are good candidates for data mining: Planning for a new product introduction, Planning direct marketing campaigns, Understanding customer attrition/churn, Evaluating results of a marketing test and allocating marketing budgets to attract the most profitable customers.

Data mining, the focus of this chapter, transforms data into actionable results. Success is about making business sense of the data, not using particular algorithms or tools. Numerous pitfalls interfere with the ability to use the results of data mining: Bad data formats, such as not including the zip code in the customer address, Confusing data fields, such as a delivery date that means "planned delivery date" in one system and "actual delivery date" in another system, Lack of functionality, such as a call-center application that does not allow annotations on a per-customer basis, Legal notifications, such as having to provide a legal reason when rejecting a loan, Organizational factors, because some operational groups are reluctant to change their operations, particularly without incentives, Lack of timeliness, because results that come too late may no longer be actionable.

Data comes in many forms, in many formats, and from multiple systems. Identifying the right data sources and bringing them together are critical success factors. Every data mining project has data issues: inconsistent systems, table keys that don't match across databases, records overwritten every few months, and so on. Complaints about data are the number one excuse for not doing anything. Data mining makes business decisions more informed. Over time, better-informed decisions are expected to have better results. The importance of measuring results has already been highlighted, although this is the stage in the virtuous cycle most likely to be overlooked. The value of measurement and continuous improvement is widely acknowledged, and yet less attention than it deserves, because it has no immediate return-on-investment. Individuals improve their own efforts by comparing and learning, by asking questions about why plans match or do not match what really happened, and by being willing to learn when and how earlier assumptions were wrong. What works for individuals also works for organizations. Data mining is a creative process. Data contains many obvious correlations that are either useless or simply represent current business policies. Data mining results change over time. Models expire and become less useful as time goes on. One cause is that data ages quickly. Markets and customers change quickly as well. Data mining provides feedback into other processes that may need to change. Decisions made in the business world often affect current processes and interactions with customers. Often, looking at data finds imperfections in operational systems, imperfections that should be fixed to enhance future customer understanding.

2.3. Knowledge Discovery in Databases

The Knowledge Discovery Process (KDP), also called knowledge discovery in databases, seeks new knowledge in some application domain. It is defined as the nontrivial process of identifying valid, novel, potentially useful, and ultimately understandable patterns in data. The process generalizes to non-database sources of data, although it emphasizes databases as a primary source of data. It consists of many steps (one of them is DM), each attempting to complete a particular discovery task and each accomplished by the application of a discovery method. Knowledge discovery concerns the entire knowledge extraction process, including how data are stored and accessed, how to use efficient and scalable algorithms to analyze massive datasets, how to interpret and visualize the results, and how to model and support the interaction between human and machine. It also concerns support for learning and analyzing the application domain.

The KDP model consists of a set of processing steps to be followed by practitioners when executing a knowledge discovery project. The model describes procedures that are performed in each of its steps. It is primarily used to plan, work through, and reduce the cost of any given project. Since the 1990s, several different KDPs have been developed. The initial efforts were led by academic research but were quickly followed by industry. The first basic structure of the model was proposed by Fayyad et al.1996 and later improved/modified by others. The process consists of multiple steps that are executed in a sequence. Each subsequent step is initiated upon successful completion of the previous step, and requires the result generated by the previous step as its input. Another common feature of the proposed models is the range of activities covered, which stretches from the task of understanding the project domain and data, through data preparation and analysis, to evaluation, understanding, and application of the generated results.

All the proposed models also emphasize the iterative nature of the model, in terms of many feedback loops that are triggered by a revision process. The main differences between the models described here lie in the number and scope of their specific steps. A common feature of all models is the definition of inputs and outputs. Typical inputs include data in various formats, such as numerical and nominal data stored in databases or flat files; images; video; semi-structured data, such as XML or HTML; etc. The output is the generated new knowledge -

usually described in terms of rules, patterns, classification models, associations, trends, statistical analysis, etc.

Although the models usually emphasize independence from specific applications and tools, they can be broadly divided into those that take into account industrial issues and those that do not. However, the academic models, which usually are not concerned with industrial issues, can be made applicable relatively easily in the industrial setting and vice versa. We restrict our discussion to those models that have been popularized in the literature and have been used in real knowledge discovery projects. The efforts to establish a KDP model were initiated in academia. In the mid-1990s, when the DM field was being shaped, researchers started defining multistep procedures to guide users of DM tools in the complex knowledge discovery world. The main emphasis was to provide a sequence of activities that would help to execute a KDP in an arbitrary domain. The (Fayyad et al.1996) KDP model consists of nine steps, which are outlined as follows: Developing and understanding the application domain includes learning the relevant prior knowledge and the goals of the end user of the discovered knowledge, Creating a target data set. Here the data miner selects a subset of variables (attributes) and data points (examples) that will be used to perform discovery tasks. This step usually includes querying the existing data to select the desired subset, Data cleaning and pre-processing consists of removing outliers, dealing with noise and missing values in the data, and accounting for time sequence information and known changes, Data reduction and projection step consists of finding useful attributes by applying dimension reduction and transformation methods, and finding invariant representation of the data, choosing the data mining task. Here the data miner matches the goals defined in 'Developing and understanding the application domain.' with a particular DM method, such as classification, regression, clustering, etc, Choosing the data mining algorithm.

The data miner selects methods to search for patterns in the data and decides which models and parameters of the methods used may be appropriate and this step generates patterns in a particular representational form such as classification rules, decision trees, regression models, trends, Interpreting mined patterns. Here the analyst performs visualization of the extracted patterns and models, and visualization of the data based on the extracted models. Consolidating discovered knowledge. The final step consists of incorporating the discovered knowledge into the performance system, and documenting and reporting it to the interested parties. This step may also include checking and resolving potential conflicts with previously believed knowledge. Industrial Model the CRISP-DM KDP (Shearer C., 2000) model consists of six steps, which are summarized below:

Business Understanding step focuses on the understanding of objectives and requirements from a business perspective. It also converts these into a DM problem definition, and designs a preliminary project plan to achieve the objectives. It is further broken into several sub steps, namely: Determination of business objectives, Assessment of the situation, Determination of DM goals, and Generation of a project plan. Data Understanding step starts with initial data collection and familiarization with the data. Specific aims include identification of data quality problems, initial insights into the data, and detection of interesting data subsets. Data understanding is further broken down into Collection of initial data, Description of data, Exploration of data and Verification of data quality.

Data Preparation step covers all activities needed to construct the final dataset, which constitutes the data that will be fed into DM tool(s) in the next step. It includes Table, record, and attribute selection, data cleaning, construction of new attributes, and transformation of data. It is divided into: Selection of data, Cleansing of data, Construction of data, Integration of data and Formatting of data sub steps. Modelling at this point, various modelling techniques are selected and applied. Modelling usually involves the use of several methods for the same DM problem type and the calibration of their parameters to optimal values. Since some methods may require a specific format for input data, often reiteration into the previous step is necessary. This step is subdivided into: Selection of modelling technique(s), Generation of test design, Creation of models and Assessment of generated models. Evaluation after one or more models have been built that have high quality from a data analysis perspective, the model is evaluated from a business objective perspective. A review of the steps executed to construct the model is also performed. A key objective is to determine whether any important business issues have not been sufficiently considered. At the end of this phase, a decision about the use of the DM results should be reached. The key sub-steps in this step include Evaluation of the results, Process review and Determination of the next step.

Deployment now the discovered knowledge must be organized and presented in a way that the customer can use. Depending on the requirements, this step can be as simple as generating a report or as complex as implementing a repeatable KDP. This step is further divided into: Plan deployment, Plan monitoring and maintenance, Generation of final report and Review of the process sub steps. Hybrid Models development of academic and industrial models has led to the development of hybrid models, i.e., models that combine aspects of both. One such model is a six-step KDP model developed by Cios et al.2000. It was developed based on the CRISP-DM model by adopting it to academic research. The main differences and extensions include providing more general, research-oriented description of the steps, Introducing a data mining step instead of the modelling step, Introducing several new explicit feedback mechanisms, (the CRISP-DM model has only three major feedback sources, while the hybrid model has more detailed feedback mechanisms) and Modification of the last step, since in the hybrid model, the knowledge discovered for a particular domain may be applied in other domains. A description of the six steps follows

Understanding of the problem domain initial step involves working closely with domain experts to define the problem and determine the project goals, identifying key people, and learning about current solutions to the problem. It also involves learning domain-specific terminology. A description of the problem, including its restrictions, is prepared. Finally, project goals are translated into DM goals, and the initial selection of DM tools to be used later in the process is performed. Understanding of the data step includes collecting sample data and deciding which data, including format and size, will be needed. Background knowledge can be used to guide these efforts. Data are checked for completeness, redundancy, missing values, plausibility of attribute values, etc. Finally, the step includes verification of the usefulness of the data with respect to the DM goals.

Preparation of the data and Data Mining step concerns deciding which data will be used as input for DM methods in the subsequent step. It involves sampling, running correlation and significance tests, and data cleaning, which includes checking the completeness of data records, removing or correcting for noise and missing values, etc. The cleaned data may be further processed by feature selection and extraction algorithms (to reduce dimensionality), by derivation of new attributes, and by summarization of data. The end results are data that meet the specific input requirements for the DM tools selected. Here the data miner uses various DM methods to derive knowledge from pre-processed data.

Evaluation of the discovered knowledge includes understanding the results, checking whether the discovered knowledge is novel and interesting, interpretation of the results by domain experts, and checking the impact of the discovered knowledge. Only approved models are retained, and the entire process is revisited to identify which alternative actions could have been taken to improve the results. A list of errors made in the process is prepared.

Use of the discovered knowledge final step consists of planning where and how to use the discovered knowledge. The application area in the current domain may be extended to other domains. A plan to monitor the implementation of the discovered knowledge is created and the entire project documented. Finally, the discovered knowledge is deployed. Most models follow a similar sequence of steps, while the common steps between the five are domain understanding, data mining, and evaluation of the discovered knowledge. The nine-step model carries out the steps concerning the choice of DM tasks and algorithms late in the process. The other models do so before pre-processing of the data in order to obtain data that are correctly prepared for the DM step without having to repeat some of the earlier steps. In the case of Fayyad's model, the prepared data may not be suitable for the tool of choice, and thus a loop back to the second, third, or fourth step may be required. The five-step model is very similar to the six-step models, except that it omits the data understanding step. The eight-step model gives a very detailed breakdown of steps in the early phases of the KDP, but it does not allow for a step concerned with applying the discovered knowledge. At the same time, it recognizes the important issue of human resource identification.

2.4.   Data Mining Task

There are different types of data mining tasks which depend on the use of data mining result, where the data mining tasks are classified as (Larose., 2005): Exploratory Data Analysis in the repositories vast amount of information's are available .This data mining task will serve the two purposes. Without the knowledge for what the customer is searching, then it analyze the data. The techniques that are said above are interactive and visual to the customer. Descriptive Modelling and Predictive Modelling. This model describes the whole data and it includes models for overall probability distribution of the data, partitioning of the p-dimensional space into groups and models describing the relationships between the variables. Evaluation of one variable is done for the prediction of other variables.

Discovering Patterns and Rules and Retrieval by Content This process is mainly done to find the hidden pattern as well as to discover the pattern in the cluster. In a cluster a number of patterns of different size and clusters are available .The main objective of this process is "how best we will detect the patterns" (Cios et al.2000). This can be achieved by using rule induction and many more techniques in the data mining algorithm like (K-Means /K-Medoids). These are known as clustering algorithm. The main aim of this method is to find the data sets of frequently used in the for audio/video as well as images It is finding pattern similar to the pattern of interest in the data set.

2.4.1.   Data Mining Applications

This section explains some of the applications of data mining and its techniques respectively (Surjeet Kumar Yadav et al, 2011). Data mining plays a vital role in healthcare industry to look into how data can be better captured, stored, prepared and mined. Possible directions include the standardization of clinical vocabulary and the sharing of data across organizations to enhance the benefits of healthcare data mining applications. When the customer wants to buying some products then this technique helps us finding the associations between different items that the customer put in their shopping buckets. Here the discovery of such associations that promotes the business technique. With huge number of higher education aspirants, it is believed that data mining technology can help bridging knowledge gap in higher educational systems. While retrieving the data from manufacturing system the customer use the data for different purposes like to find the errors in the data, to enhance the design methodology, to make the good quality of the data ,how best the data can be supported for making the decision. A data in one context is very important may not be much important in other context. A context-aware data-mining framework filters useful and interesting context factors, and can produce accurate and precise prediction using those factors.

Credit scoring has become very important issue due to the recent growth of the credit industry, so the credit department of the bank faces the huge numbers of consumer's credit data to process, but it is impossible analyzing this huge amount of data both in economic and manpower terms. Diagnosis of disease, health care, patient profiling and history generation etc. are the few examples. Mammography is the method used in breast cancer detection. Radiologists face lot of difficulties in detection of tumour's that's why CAM (Computer Aided Methods) could helps to the medical staff. The classification method of data mining is used to classify the network traffic normal traffic or abnormal traffic. In the sports world the vast amounts of statistics are collected for each player, team, game, and season. In the game sports the data's are available in the form of statistical form where data mining can be used and discover the patterns, these patterns are often used to predict the future forecast. The Intelligence Agencies collect and analyze information to investigate terrorist activities.

The data mining system implemented at the Internal Revenue Service to identify high-income individuals engaged in abusive tax shelters show significantly good results.

E-commerce is also the most prospective domain for data mining. It is ideal because many of the ingredients required for successful data mining are easily available: data records are plentiful, electronic collection provides reliable data, insight can easily be turned into action, and return on investment can be measured. The data mining application can be used in the field of the Digital Library where the user will finds or collects, stores and preserves the data which are in the form of digital mode. The prediction problems like the cost estimation problem in engineering, the problem of engineering design that involves decisions where parameters, actions, components, and so on are selected.

Data mining technique is used for the variety of the parameters in the field of engineering applications like prior data. Both practitioners and academics use data mining techniques in customer relation management to decrease the churn prediction and increase the number of customer to gain the maximum profit in the market.

2.5.   Summary

This chapter provided the introduction on data mining, kinds of collection of information, need for data mining, how to transform data into information, knowledge discovery in databases, data mining task and data mining applications. The next chapter discusses customer relation management and churning of customer.

CHAPTER 3

CUSTOMER RELATIONSHIP MANAGEMENT

3.1. Introduction

Today, many businesses such as banks, insurance companies, and other service providers realize the importance of Customer Relationship Management (CRM) and its potential to help them acquire new customers retain existing ones and maximize their lifetime value. At this point, close relationship with customers will require a strong coordination between IT and marketing departments to provide a long-term retention of selected customers. This chapter deals with the role of Customer Relationship Management in banking sector and the need for Customer Relationship Management to increase customer value by using analytical methods in CRM applications which is churn prediction.

CRM is a sound business strategy to identify the bank's most profitable customers and prospects, and devotes time and attention to expanding account relationships with those customers through individualized marketing, reprising, discretionary decision making, and customized service-all delivered through the various sales channels that the bank uses. Under this case study, a campaign management in a bank is conducted using data mining tasks such as dependency analysis, cluster profile analysis, concept description, deviation detection, and data visualization. Crucial business decisions with this campaign are made by extracting valid, previously unknown and ultimately comprehensible and actionable knowledge from large databases.

The model developed here answers what the different customer segments are, who more likely to respond to a given offer is, which customers are the bank likely to lose, which most likely to default on credit cards is, what the risk associated with this loan applicant. Finally, a cluster profile analysis is used for revealing the distinct characteristics of each cluster, and for modelling product propensity, which should be implemented in order to increase the sales. The idea of CRM is that it helps businesses use technology and human resources gain insight into the behaviour of customers and the value of those customers. If it works as hoped, a business can provide better customer service, Make call centres more efficient, Cross sell products more effectively, Help sales staff close deals faster, Simplify marketing and sales processes, Discover new customers, Increase customer revenues. The above mentioned things don't get happen by simply buying software and installing it.

For CRM to be truly effective an organization must first decide what kind of customer information it is looking for and it must decide what it intends to do with that information. For example, many financial institutions keep track of customers' life stages in order to market appropriate banking products like mortgages or IRAs to them at the right time to fit their needs. Next, the organization must look into all of the different ways information about customers comes into a business, where and how this data is stored and how it is currently used. One company, for instance, may interact with customers in a myriad of different ways including mail campaigns, Web sites, brick-and-mortar stores, call centers, mobile sales force staff and marketing and advertising efforts. Solid CRM systems link up each of these points. This collected data flows between operational systems (like sales and inventory systems) and analytical systems that can help sort through these records for patterns.

Company analysts can then comb through the data to obtain a holistic view of each customer and pinpoint areas where better services are needed. In CRM projects, following data should be collected to run process engine: 1) Responses to campaigns, 2) Shipping and fulfilment dates, 3) Sales and purchase data, 4) Account information, 5) Web registration data, 6) Service and support records, 7) Demographic data, 8) Web sales data. This chapter provides introduction to customer relationship management, several research dimensions of customer relationship management classification framework, prediction of churners. Also this chapter reviews traditional methods used for prediction and the other traditional models used for classification of churn behaviour.

3.2. Customer Relationship Management

Customer Relationship Management (CRM) is a concept that middles on transforming the relationship between a firm and its customers by developing a one-to-one relationship. In examining the domain of CRM, three perspectives are dominant. The first relates to a better understanding of the customer base by identifying various customer segments and gaining knowledge on their needs.

The second perspective involves opening up different channels of communication to enable the customer to access products and services whenever they want. The last perspective hinges on building a knowledge base of information required to provide services by aggregating customer interaction data to offer the customer an enhanced service experience. As CRM systems play a pivotal role in supporting such customer relationship strategies, it is important to delineate the domain of these systems.

CRM is based on RM and is focused on the technology underlying the management of customers. CRM has its origin in the desire of combining the help desk, the customer support, the ERP and data mining. The first CRM initiatives were launched in the early 1990s and were mainly focused on call that middles the activities. The promising emergence of CRM was influenced by the advances in information technologies, data management systems, improved analytics, enhanced communications, systems integration and internet adoption. Currently, in information technology terms, CRM means the integration of technologies such as: data warehouse, website, intranet/extranet, help desk, sales, accounting, ERP and data mining. Indeed, all information technology able to gather data is integrated in order to provide the information required to create a more personal interaction with customers.

CRM can be defined as the process of using information technology in implementing relationship marketing strategies, with particular emphasis on customer relationships. Nairn, (2002) defined CRM as a long-term business philosophy that focuses on collecting and understanding customer information, treating different customers differently, providing a higher level of service for the best customers and using these together to increase customer loyalty and profitability. Customer relationship management (CRM) having processes along with enabling systems which fortifies a business strategy to build long term, remuneratively lucrative relationships with categorical customers. Customer data and Information Technology (IT) implements form the substructure upon which any prosperous CRM strategy is built.

Supplemental to the above, the expeditious elevate of the Internet and its associated technologies have greatly incremented the opportunities for marketing and has transformed the way relationships between companies and their customers are managed. While CRM has become widely recognized as an important business approach, there is no universally accepted definition of CRM (Ngai, 2005). CRM an "enterprise approach to understanding and determining the customer behaviour through meaningful communications in order to improve customer acquisition, customer retention, customer loyalty, and customer profitability". CRM is viewed as "the strategic use of information, processes, technology, and people to manage the customer's relationship with your company across the whole customer life cycle". Parvatiyar and Sheth, (2002) defined CRM as "a comprehensive strategy and process of acquiring, retaining, and partnering with selective customers to create superior value for the company and the customer. It involves the integration of marketing, sales, customer service, and the supply chain functions of the organization to achieve greater efficiencies and effectiveness in delivering customer value". These definitions emphasize the importance of viewing CRM as a comprehensive process of acquiring and retaining customers, with the help of business intelligence, to maximize the customer value to the organization.

From the architecture point of view, the CRM framework can be classified into operational and analytical (Teo et al., 2006). Operational CRM refers to the automation of business processes. Analytical CRM refers to the analysis of customer characteristics and behaviours so as to support the organization's customer management strategies. As such, analytical CRM could help an organization to better discriminate and more effectively allocate resources to the most profitable group of customers. Data mining tools are a popular means of analyzing customer data with- in the analytical CRM framework. Many organizations have collected and stored a wealth of data about their current customers, potential customers, suppliers and business partners. On the other hand, the inability to discover valuable information hidden in the data prevents the organizations from transforming these data into valuable and useful knowledge. Data mining tools could help these organizations to discover the hidden knowledge in the enormous amount of data.

Turban et al., (2007) defined data mining as "the process that uses statistical, mathematical, artificial intelligence and machine-learning techniques to extract and identify useful information and subsequently gain knowledge from large databases". Having voluminous customer data, data mining technology can provide business intelligence to generate new opportunities. The application of data mining tasks and effective algorithm in CRM is a thrust area of research. The foundation of development of such CRM is based on analyzing and understanding customer behaviours and characteristics. This is done in order to acquire and retain potential customers and maximize customer value. Apt data mining algorithms that are good at extracting and identifying useful information and knowledge from enormous customer databases are one of the best supporting tools for making CRM decisions. As such, the application of data mining techniques in CRM is worth pursuing in a customer-centric economy. As the nature of research in CRM and data mining are difficult to confine to specific disciplines, the relevant materials are scattered across various journals. Business intelligence and knowledge discovery is the most common academic discipline for data mining research in CRM.

3.2.1. *Dimensions of CRM*

There are four dimensions in CRM which are

- Customer Identification
- Customer Attraction
- Customer Retention
- Customer Development

These four dimensions can be seen as a closed cycle of a customer management system. Hence data mining techniques will accomplish the goal of extracting or detecting hidden customer characteristics and behaviours from large databases. The generative aspect of data mining consists of the building of a model from data. Each data mining technique can perform one or more of the following types of data modelling: Association, Classification, Clustering, Forecasting, Regression, Sequence discovery and Visualization. The seven models are commonly mentioned data mining models in articles (Ahmed, 2004, Turban et al., 2007). There are numerous machine learning techniques available for each type of data mining model. Choices of data mining techniques should be based on the data characteristics and business requirements.

Some commonly used data mining algorithms are:

- Association rule
- Decision tree
- Genetic algorithm
- Neural networks
- K-Nearest neighbour
- Linear/logistic regression

CRM is helping organization to better discriminate and more effectively allocate resources to the most profitable group of customers through the cycle of customer identification, customer attraction, and customer retention and customer development. The four dimensions of the CRM cycles are essential efforts to gain customer handy. Customer Identification CRM begins with this dimension also called customer acquisition. Customer identification includes mainly customer segmentation and target customer analysis. Customer segmentation implies the subdivision of the set of all customers into smaller segments including customers with similar characteristics. Target customer analysis involves the definition of the most attractive segments for the company, based on customer's characteristics. The selection of the target groups requires the collection of quantitative and qualitative data on these groups.

Customer Attraction follows customers' identification. Having identified the target groups, companies concentrate efforts and allocate resources to attract these segments. Competitive advantages, such as price and other differentiation characteristics, can be drivers of customers' attraction. Another customer attraction driver is direct marketing. This is an element of company's marketing mix that motivates customers to place an order immediately. For instance, direct mail or coupon distribution is typical examples of direct marketing. Customer attraction involves the use of an appropriate method of communication and the elimination of any sort of wasted effort. Customer Retention dimension is one of the main concerns of CRM. Customer satisfaction is the main issue regarding customers' retention. Customer satisfaction can be defined as the comparison of customers' expectations with the perceptions (resulting from actual experience, subjective impression of product performance, appropriateness of the product or service, etc). The customer's perception of the value offered by the company leads to sustained customer retention. Moreover, a high quality shopping experience leads to a positive emotional feeling, which enables the company to achieve the desired customer loyalty. Elements of this CRM dimension include one-to-one marketing, loyalty and bonus programs, and complaints management. One-to-one marketing involves personalized marketing campaigns supported by analyzing, detecting and predicting changes in customer behaviour. Loyalty and bonus programs involve campaigns or supporting activities which aim at maintaining a long term relationship with customers. Examples of loyalty programs include credit scoring, service quality or satisfaction and churn analysis, i.e. analysis whether a customer is likely to leave for a competitor.

Customer Development involves consistent expansion of transaction intensity, transaction value and individual customer profitability. Elements of customer development include customer lifetime value analysis, up/cross selling and market basket analysis. Customer lifetime value analysis is defined as the prediction of the total net income a company can expect from a customer. Up/Cross selling refers to promotion activities which aim at augmenting the number of associated or closely related services that a customer uses within a firm (Prinzie & Poel, 2006). Market basket analysis aims at maximizing the customer transaction intensity and value by revealing regularities in the purchase behaviour of customers.

3.2.2. *Classification Framework-Data Mining Models*

Within the context of CRM, data mining can be seen as a business driven process aimed at the discovery and consistent use of profitable knowledge from organizational data. It can be used to guide decision making and fore-cast the effects of decisions. For instance, data mining can in- crease the response rates of the marketing campaign by segmenting customers into groups with different characteristics and needs; it can predict how likely an existing customer is to take his/her business to a competitor. Each of the CRM elements can be supported by different data mining models, which generally include association, classification, clustering, forecasting, regression, sequence discovery and visualization. Association aims to establishing relationships between items which exist together in a given record (Zhang et al., 2009). Market basket analysis and cross selling programs are typical examples for which association modelling is usually adopted. Common tools for association modelling are statistics and apriori algorithms. Classification is one of the most common learning models in data mining. It aims at building a model to predict future customer behaviours through classifying file records into a number of predefined classes based on certain criteria. Common tools used for classifications are neural networks, decision trees and if- then-else rules.

Clustering is the task of segmenting a heterogeneous population into a number of more homogenous clusters. It is different to classification in that clusters are unknown at the time the algorithm starts. In other words, there are no predefined clusters. Common tools for clustering include neural networks and discrimination analysis. Forecasting estimates the future value based on a record's patterns. It deals with continuously valued out- comes. It relates to modelling and the logical relationships of the model at some time in the future. Demand forecast is a typical example of a forecasting model. Common tools for forecasting include neural networks and survival analysis.

Regression is a kind of statistical estimation technique used to map each data object to a real value provide prediction value. Uses of regression include curve fitting, prediction, modelling of causal relationships, and testing scientific hypotheses about relationships between variables. Common tools for regression include linear regression and logistic regression. Sequence discovery is the identification of associations or patterns over time. Its goal is to model the states of the process generating the sequence or to extract and report deviation and trends over time. Common tools for sequence discovery are statistics and set theory. Visualization refers to the presentation of data so that users can view complex patterns. It is used in conjunction with other data mining models to provide a clearer understanding of the discovered patterns or relationships. Examples of visualization model are 3D graphs, "Hygraphs" and "SeeNet".

A combination of data mining algorithms is often required to support or forecast the effects of a CRM strategy. In such a situation, the classification of data mining models mentioned in the article will be based on the major CRM issues that the article would like to address. For instance, in the case of up/cross selling programs, customers can be segmented into clusters before an association model is applied to each cluster. In such cases, the up/cross selling program would be classified as being supported by an association model because relationships between products are the major concern; in the case of direct marketing, a certain portion of customers may be segmented into clusters to form the initial classes of the classification model. The direct marketing program would be classified as being supported by classification as prediction of customers' behaviour is the major concern.

3.3. Churn Prediction

Customer churn is a major concern for businesses in competitive industries. It is well established that investments in customer retention provide far greater return on investment than campaigns to attract new customers. The difficulty comes in identifying those customers who are likely to churn and in targeting them with appropriate retention programs. As a first step, businesses gather information on customer demographics, prior transaction history, and service-related factors based on contacts (e.g., business transactions).

As these customer information repositories grow massive over time businesses are challenged to turn the information into actionable operations, due in part to a lack of understanding of effective analytic methods for "sensing and responding" to the patterns found in the data. Thus, managers sometimes question huge investments in Customer Relationship Management (CRM) systems and data warehouses due to a lack of direct operational consequences. It is becoming common knowledge in business, that retaining existing customers is the best core marketing strategy to survive in industry (Kim and Street, 2004, Lariviere and Van Den poel, 2004). Retained customers generate more financial returns than new customers, which is why businesses should make every effort to retain their existing customer base, rather than investing valuable revenue in attempting to capture new subscribers (Buckinx et al., 2004).

Many researchers expanded this by claiming "in addition to the reduced costs, there is potential and opportunity value of customers which is gained over a long period of time. In order to be successful in the maturing market, the strategic focus of a company ought to shift from acquiring customers to retaining customers by reducing customer churn". Further to the increase of sales and profits that are generated by loyal customers it has also become apparent that when a customer churns from his/her current service provider costs are imposed on that service provider that are in most cases unrecoverable. Churn is the term that has been adopted to define the movement of customers from one provider to another, and churn management is the process of the operator's efforts to retain those customers. These efforts usually involve the deployment of proactive retention campaigns in a bid to win the customers business before that business is lost (Hung et al., 2006). When the number of customers belonging to a specific service industry reaches its peak, finding and securing new customers becomes increasingly difficult and costly. At this point of the businesses lifecycle it should be higher priority to retain existing customers than trying to win new ones. It is also very difficult for a company to attempt to win new business. This is because the process of winning new business often involves offering attractive introductory packages. These packages are usually not available to existing customers which can cause animosity, resulting in decreased customer satisfaction levels. Further to this, existing customers might move to competitors to themselves take advantage of new customer offers, due to the fact that they cannot qualify for them through their existing service provider.

Churning customers can be divided into two main groups, voluntary churners and non-voluntary churners. Non-voluntary churn is the type of churn in which the service is purposely withdrawn by the company. There are several reasons why a company could revoke a customer's service. Reasons such as abuse of service and non-payment of service is usually the main causes. Voluntary churn is more difficult to determine. This type of churn occurs when a customer makes a conscious decision to terminate his/her service with the provider. This type of churn has been a serious and puzzling problem for service providers. The varied behaviour of consumers has baffled the researchers. Voluntary churn can be divided into two sub categories, incidental churn and deliberate churn. Incidental churn happens when changes in circumstances prevent the customer from further requiring the provided service. Examples of incidental churn include changes in the customer's financial circumstances so that the customer can no longer afford the service, or a move to a different geographical location where the company's service is unavailable. Incidental churn usually only explains a small percentage of a company's voluntary churn. This type of churn is also known as 'financial churn' (Burez and Van Den Poel, 2009).

A churn management solution should not target the entire customer base because (i) not all customers are worth retaining, and (ii) customer retention costs money attempting to retain customers that have no intention of churning is a waste of resources. Companies need to understand their customers. Liu and Shih, (2005) reinforced this statement by suggesting that intense competition is forcing organisations to develop novel marketing strategies to capture customer needs in an attempt to improve satisfaction and retention. It states that trying to sell more to everyone is no longer a profitable sales strategy and a market place that continually grows more competitive requires an approach that focuses on the most efficient use of sales resources. It is further reinforced that "the profit impact of customer retention has become accepted wisdom".

Finding a suitable measurement of customer satisfaction is a major problem for organisations and has been a focus of research for quite some time. Measuring customer satisfaction is a major problem for every firm or organisation, especially within the frame of marketing management practices. Satisfaction of customer needs is the main objective according to the principles of modern marketing science. The importance of customer satisfaction has been accepted, and has received attention from researchers across multiple service sectors. Some examples include determining customer satisfaction levels in the context of online retailing E-Commerce (Liu and Shiih, 2005), Construction Project Management (CPM) which is a technically an oriented service for construction project clients (Yang and Padmanabhan, 2005),and customer satisfaction levels within the telecommunications industry.

Companies should be continuously improving their products and services to retain and enhance customer satisfaction; however customer satisfaction can suffer from other areas of business such as customer service, billing problems and faults. Seeking to maintain customer satisfaction through a product based approach alone is insufficient. Improving the range of products and enhancing services does not necessarily improve customer satisfaction levels, however poor product availability and bad service can have a high negative impact on customer satisfaction. This suggests that although services and technologies need to be up-to-date from a strategic point of view, service errors are more damaging than service upgrades are rewarding, in terms of existing customer perceptions.

Customer loyalty is regarded in industry to be different to customer satisfaction. Loyal customers have been described as customers who show a psychological reaction and conviction to a specific product or service experience. Loyal customers are believed to possess a positive mental attitude towards their service provider, executing a continued repurchase conduct. Customer loyalty is not a new concept in business. In fact it was realised that repeat purchasing from existing customers was crucial to business strategy as early back as 1942. Customer loyalty is more prevalent in service type businesses rather than product type businesses have determined that in the case of the telecommunications industry satisfaction explains nearly 100% of customers loyalty. This supports who state that the concept of customer value is related to, but different from, that of satisfaction. The literature identifies two types of satisfactions: transactional and overall satisfaction (or cumulative satisfaction).

Transactional satisfaction is defined as post choice evaluative judgment of a specific purchase occasion, whereas cumulative customer satisfaction is an overall evaluation based on the total experience. The main benefits that are unique and common to loyal customers have been recognized by research performed by who claim that repeat buying, immunity to competing offers and complaining behaviour are all traits of customer loyalty. The concept of customer loyalty has received multiple definitions and interpretations. Researchers holding a deterministic view, generally regard loyalty from an attitudinal perspective, while researchers holding a stochastic view tend to regard loyalty from a behavioural perspective. For example, word of mouth has been used in some cases as a dimension of loyalty by some researchers and an outcome of loyalty by others. Researchers have since taken the view of combining both loyalty views, to create a multidimensional view of loyalty, including a broad range of loyal states to benefit both the customer and the marketer. Examples of the dimensions of loyalties are as follows:

Situational Loyalty has been regarded that loyalty could be the result of situations faced over time, and as a tendency for a person to exhibit similar behaviour. To elaborate, situational loyalty is the understanding that customers purchase products depending on the situation, such as purchasing a gift for an anniversary etc. Resistance to competing offers one example of a customer that would be resistant would be a customer who is contracted to a supplier, making them unable to respond to competing offers. The relationship between resistance to competing offers and loyalty is still unclear. Again, some researchers regard resistance to competing offers as a dimension of loyalty, while others regard it as a consequence. Propensity to be loyal is regarded as an important measure for marketers, because it is regarded that it can sound the alarm for a decline in other loyal states. Measures of attitudinal loyalty include preference, intention to repurchase, and commitment. Attitudinal loyalty is usually used for predicting behaviour. Word of mouth has been used by some research as a measure of attitudinal loyalty. Complaining behaviour may appear strange to include complaining behaviour and aspect of customer loyalty, however researchers view complaining behaviour as the customer using his/her voice', and it is regarded that complaints can provide positive feedback to a company as well as negative. Some researchers view complaining behaviour as a dimension of loyalty, while other researchers view it as a consequence of loyalty.

3.4.   Traditional Methods

This section covers the most common techniques that have been commonly used for predictive analysis and data mining. Decision Tree is the most popular type of predictive model and has become an important knowledge structure, used for the classification of future events (Rosset et al., 2002). Decision Tree development usually consists of two phases, tree building and tree pruning. The tree-building phase consists of recursively partitioning the training sets according to the values of the attributes. The partitioning process continues until all, or most of the records in each of the partitions contain identical values. Certain branches may need to be removed because it is possible that they could consist of noisy data. The pruning phase involves selecting and removing the branches that contain the largest estimated error rate. Tree pruning is known to enhance the predictive accuracy of the decision tree while reducing complexity. Pruning should be regarded as a process of experimentation because it is possible that pruning the tree could decrease the accuracy of the output rather than enhance it. The C5.0 classification tree assembles classification trees by recursively splitting the instance space into smaller subgroups until only instances from the same class remain. These instances are known as pure nodes. Likewise, sub-groups containing occurrences from different classes are known as impure nodes. The tree is allowed to grow to its full potential before it is pruned back in order to increase its power of generalisation on unseen data (Au et al., 2003).

A Classification and Regression Tree (CART) is constructed by recursively splitting the instance space into smaller sub-groups until a specified criterion has been met. The decrease in impurity of the parent node against the child nodes defines the goodness of the split. The tree is only allowed to grow until the decrease in impurity falls below a user-defined threshold. At this time the node becomes terminal, or leaf node. Chen et al., (2003) used a decision tree based approach to propose a model for customer profile analysis. The customer base was first segmented into groups of customers that were labelled as preferred and regular, the preferred customers being those most valuable to the company.

The decision tree was then applied to the segments in order to determine the necessary measures to take for both the preferred and regular divisions, aiming to prevent customers from switching to alternative companies. Dividing a population of data and generating nodes using optional explanatory variables creates the decision tree. Hwang et al., (2004) performed experiments by involving a decision tree, a neural network and logistic regression. The decision tree showed slightly better accuracy over the other technologies; however, this states that these results do not prove decision trees to be the best choice in all cases. This is supported by Mozer et al, (2000) and suggested that for the purpose of customer retention, the feature selection process has to be accurate. For the purpose of identifying potential defectors they chose a C4.5 classification method. This is a decision tree induction method for classification because it has shown a proven good performance and it automatically generates classification rules.

Keaveney and Parthasarathy, (2001) used an exploratory methodology the study surveyed 500 individuals for "critical incidents," where a critical incident represents any encounter between a customer and a firm that causes the customer to switch providers. The top two categories of factors, which appeared in 30% to 40% of the sample, were "core service failures" and "service encounter failures." Core service failures were obvious errors such as billing errors or a package delivered late. Service encounter failures relate to perceived issues in the actual interactions between customers and service providers (e.g., "the doctor was curt" or "the representative seemed rude"). The next two categories were pricing and inconvenience factors (e.g., "customer service is not 24 hours"). A key contribution of the study which was done by Keaveney and Parthasarathy, (2001) demonstrated a link between service quality and subsequent customer responses. An important finding was that service factors seem paramount and even dwarf pricing considerations when customers chose service providers. Since the study, a variety of articles, mostly in the fields of marketing and operations, have addressed churn with the goal of identifying the drivers of churn. While demographics, pricing, competition, varying product features, and natural reasons (e.g., upgrading to a luxury brand with wealth increase) have all been demon- started to be important, customer satisfaction and service quality (Graves et al., 1998) remain two critical factors that have received particular attention. In addition to their intrinsic importance, businesses often have direct control on such factors, making an active response possible. Rust et al, (1995) coined the term "return on quality" to reject the importance of investing in service quality. Buckinx and Poel, (2004) classified prior churn research until 2005 based on use of three categories of predictor variables: prior behaviour, demographics, and perceptions (e.g., customer surveys).

Regression Analysis is a popular technique used by the researchers dealing with predicting customer satisfaction. It provides a first step of model development. A new model for assessing the value of customer satisfaction was developed by Rust et al, (1995). They used logistic regression to link satisfaction with attributes of customer retention. They claim that the logistic function can be interpreted as providing the retention probability. Hwang et al, (2004) discovered that logistic regression performed best for predicting customer churn when compared with neural networks and decision tree. It should be noted the authors were investigating a prediction of the Customer Lifetime Value (CLV), with the intent of including customer churn; they suggest that logistic regression was the best model for their purpose. The authors believe that many factors could influence these results such as the neural network parameters chosen and the data that the experiment was based on. The data used for experimentation may have been more suited to a logistic regression model than that of a neural network or decision tree. Drew et al, (2001) used simple regression to initially predict churn but later experimented with KNN, decision trees and neural networks. The overall model used to develop the churn prediction platform was done using a neural network. Their research could not establish a best method. They have stated future directions as including an explanation of customer behaviour because their model was unable to predict customer churn accurately. The model suggested by Drew et al, (2001) fails to distinguish between loyal customers, valuable customers and less profitable customers. They suggest that future research should include a more financial orientated approach by optimising payoff. They further suggest that by concentrating on payoff rather than churn the developed model would weight those customers bringing in higher profits over those bringing in lesser profits.

Soft computing is a consortium of methodologies (such as fuzzy logic, neural networks, and genetic algorithms) that work synergistically and provides, in one form or another, flexible information processing capabilities for handling case problems. Exploiting the tolerance for imprecision, uncertainty, approximate reasoning and partial truth in order to achieve tractability, robustness, low solution cost, and close resemblance with human-like decision making is the aim of soft computing. Technologies that fall in the category of soft computing are Evolutionary Computation (EC), Artificial Neural Networks (NN), Fuzzy Logic (FL), Probabilistic Computing (PC) and their combinations, for example, Neuro-Fuzzy Systems. Evolutionary Computing consists of various computational techniques that have been inspired and developed on the evolution theory as proposed by Charles Darwin. He was one of the leading intellectuals of 18th century England who proposed in his publication On the Origin of Species by Means of Natural Selection', that evolution was an inevitable process through the mechanism of natural selection and survival of the fittest. These theories of natural selection and survival of the fittest have been computationally mimicked to effectively solve real life problems in the forms of such techniques as Genetic Programming (GP) and Genetic Algorithms (GA).

GA is an evolutionary computing technique that is used to solve optimisation problems. An initial population made up of as chromosomes (solutions) is randomly generated. Each part of the chromosome is known as a gene and the chromosomes are used to spawn new generation through crossover and mutation operators. The fitness of each solution (chromosome) is evaluated against a specific fitness function. The fittest of these chromosomes are selected to become the parent solutions and the whole process repeats. This process can run over hundreds or thousands of generations depending on the complexity of the problem, and eventually the near optimum solution is reached. Other Traditional Methods proposed by Prinzie and Van Den Poel, (2008) introduced a Mixture Transition Distribution (MTD) to investigate purchase-sequence patterns. The MTD is designed to allow estimations of high order Markov chains, providing a smaller transition matrix facilitating managerial interpretation. Markov chains were also used for relationship marketing to obtain an estimation of the Customer's Lifetime Value (CLV).

There are five firm-level variables named as customer Satisfaction Index Scores (SAT), Customer Loyalty Index Scores (LOY), Year of Data (YEAR), Relative Quality Importance (RQI) and the average ease of comparing quality differences, to create a general linear model. (Prinzie and Van Den Poel., 2006) do not offer a precise explanation of how these variables were selected; the authors have determined the following definitions from the literature. SAT has been defined as a cumulative evaluation of a customer's purchase and consumption habits. YEAR represents the year that the data is relevant. RQI determines the relative impact that the perceived quality and value has on customer satisfaction. Estimations were established using a model based on quality-versus-price as defined by the American customer satisfaction index model.

EQ is defined as a measure of the ease of judging and comparing quality. It is the average of the response collected by asking the following question: "Thinking about the quality of the product (e.g. mobile telephones) do you consider it easy or difficult to judge what is high versus low quality?" This question would have a score ranging between 1 and 10. A score of 1 would represent very easy while a score of 10 would represent very difficult. LOY is an indication of the customer's intentions to repurchase services or goods. Regression was used as an alternative to test for linear equality restrictions. Support Vector Machine (SVM) is another technology that is worth investigating for its suitability for use with customer churn management; however a thorough search of the literature has revealed little investigation into this method. The closest research to CRM identified by the author is the mining of customer credit scores. This research used regression trees as a final model; however SVM was also investigated. The paper states that the SVM approach has emerged as a new and promising approach for the process of data classification. The technology is described as methodical and inspired by statistical learning theory. The experiments performed in the research took advantage of Matlab's SVM toolbox. The experiments showed similar results to neural networks. It is documented that on a standard PC, it took roughly 20 hours to analyse a dataset of 8000 records, suggesting a major drawback of the technology (Ahn et al., 2006).

3.5.   Summary

This chapter provided the customer relationship management introduction, dimensions of CRM classification framework, churn prediction, traditional methods used for prediction and the other traditional model used for prediction. The next chapter discusses class imbalance and customer churn prediction through class imbalance.

CHAPTER 4

CHURN PREDICTION AND CLASS IMBALANCE

4.1. Introduction

Customer churn and engagement has become one of the top issues for most banks. It costs significantly more to acquire new customers than retain existing ones and it costs far more to reacquire defected customers. In fact, several empirical studies and models have proven that churn remains one of the biggest destructors of enterprise value for banks and other consumer intensive companies. Churn has an equal or greater impact on Customer Lifetime Value when compared to one of the most regarded KPI's (Key Performance Indicator) such as ARPU (Average Revenue per User). The quality of service and banking fees seem to be the top two drivers for customers to consider another alternative.

In today's networked economy, every poor customer experience, or seemingly unfair fee, can snowball into a shift in customer sentiment, risk of churn and major revenue loss. In today's interconnected world, bad news spreads rapidly via exploding social media interactions that reflect customer sentiment as well as influence the sentiment of others. Many leading banks get anywhere between 10,000 to hundreds and thousands of social medias are simplified within 30 days.

The ability to track customer sentiment gives bank's early indicators into customer service issues or pricing issues. It also allows banks to be proactive in improving the customer's experience, their engagement with the brand, and saves significant downstream costs and revenues losses. However, the information about a customer's sentiment and their experience across multiple channels lies in many structured and unstructured data sources. The information could be in the form of logs from a customer's bank visits, website interactions, call center logs, tweets, facebook interactions, community forums, customer e-mails, and customer surveys. More importantly the information is almost always locked within functional and application silos. This makes it challenging for the banks to get a holistic understanding of their customers, understand the shift in the sentiment or detect early warning signs and proactively engage them with retention or cross-sell marketing offers. In order to identify early signs of potential churn you first need to start getting a holistic 360-degree view of your customers and their interactions across multiple channels such as bank visits, calls to customer service departments, Web-based transactions, mobile banking and social media interactions.

Customers who possess only one banking product such as a checking account, decrease in the assets in a customer's accounts, Sale of one or more financial products such as loans, stocks or bonds, cancellation of automatic incoming credits or outgoing payments, negative customer interactions on customer calls, drop off in web-based banking activities, drop off in mobile payments and the value of mobile transactions and customer complaints about specific issues on social media.

There are several key limitations of traditional technologies, which are inhibitors for gaining, a holistic, 360-degree view of customers: A bank's ability to store transactional data is fairly restricted due to storage and retrieval limitations. You can only store information for a short time interval, the cost of storing large volumes of data becomes prohibitive if you are using traditional technologies, the inability to manage unstructured and semi-structured data– which is growing the fastest and does provide the most real-time insights about customer sentiments or early warning signs, without sophisticated data matching, simply storing data into a single platform does not unlock the information from application or functional silos. It does not connect the dots to identify all interactions of a unique customer across multiple channels. Batch-mode analytics provides an outdated view of customers and their sentiments. It often becomes too late for retention programs to be effective. There is a lot of incomplete information (the Veracity problem) about the customer that is being generated across multiple channels and it becomes very difficult to account for this incomplete information and turn it into meaningful insights.

This chapter details gives an introduction to churn predication. The types of churn, common methodologies used for churn prediction, research dimensions in churn prediction, the value of lifetime of customers, class imbalance problem which is the general scenario in CRM research, multiclass imbalance and finally boosting algorithms in class imbalance research problem. The rapid growth of the market in every sector is leading to a bigger subscriber base for service providers. More competitors, new and innovative business models and better services are increasing the cost of customer acquisition. In this environment service providers have realized the importance of the retention of existing customers. Therefore, providers are forced to put more efforts for prediction and prevention of churn. It is most commonly used data mining techniques for the identification of churn. Based on historical data these methods try to find patterns which can point out possible churners. Well-known techniques used for this are Regression analysis, Decision Trees, Neural Networks and Rule based learning.

4.2.   Customer Churn

'Churn' is a word derived from change and turn. It means the discontinuation of a contract. There are three types of churn: Active/Deliberate: customer decides to quit his contract and to switch to another provider. Reasons for this may include unsatisfaction with the quality of service (e.g. not fulfilling service level agreements), Too high costs, not competitive price plans, no rewards for customer loyalty, no understanding of the service scheme, bad support, no information about reasons and predicted resolution time for service problems, no continuity or fault resolution, privacy concerns, etc. Rotational/incidental: the customer quits contract without the aim of switching to a competitor. Reasons for this is changes in the circumstances that prevent the customer from further requiring the service, e.g. financial problems, leading to impossibility of payment; or change of the geographical location of the customer to a place where the company is not present or the service is unavailable. Passive/ Non-voluntary: the company discontinues the contract itself. Voluntary churn (active, rotational) is hard to predict. And while incidental churn only explains a small fraction of overall churn it is particularly interesting to predict and react taking appropriate action to prevent deliberate churn. In order to prevent customers' voluntary contract discontinuation, however, the company needs to know who possible churners is and with a low probability of error in the prediction and why this specific customer has decided to leave the company for the benefit of a competitor. Furthermore, churning can be divided also in three other groups: Total - the agreement is officially cancelled. Hidden-the contract is not cancelled, but the customer is not actively using the service since a long period of time. Partial-the agreement is not cancelled, but the customer is not using the services to a full extent and is using only parts of it, and is instead using constantly a service of a competitor.

Depending on the company, the contract type and the business model that is being applied hidden or partial churning can lead to considerable money loss (e.g. in telecommunications: the customer only pays the monthly subscription fee, but does not place a single call) and also needs to be identified and action should be taken in order not to lose completely the customer. Moreover, it is important to classify which of the possible churners are of further interest for the company, e.g. which customers are likely to generate more profit (these are typically customers who generated substantial revenues and then found a better offer with a good loyalty programme at a competitor), and which customers are not interesting, because, for instance, they are identified as risky. Then the company marketing department can consider direct marketing strategies in order to retain important customers. Churn is an unavoidable phenomenon, but it can be managed and the potential losses to the business can be minimized.

The timely detection of possible churners, together with effective retention efforts supports this goal. In a world of ever growing competition on the market, companies have become aware that they should put much effort not only trying to convince customers to sign contracts, but also to retain existing clients. Den Pole and Lariviere, (2004) have shown that in the current setting where people are given a huge choice of offers and different service providers to decide upon, winning new customers is a costly and hard process. Therefore, putting more effort in keeping churn low has become essential for service-oriented companies.

Den Poel and Lariviere, (2004) summarized the economic value of customer retention: lowering the need to seek new and potentially risky customers, which allows focusing on the demands of existing customers, long-term customers tend to buy more, positive word of mouth from satisfied customers is a good way for new customers' acquisition, long-term customers are less costly to serve, because of a larger database of their demands, long-term customers are less sensitive to competitors' marketing activities, losing customers results in less sales and an increased need to attract new customers, which is five to six times more expensive than the money spent for retention of existing customers, People tend to share more often negative than positive service experience with friends, resulting in negative image of the company among possible future customers. Customer Relationship Management (CRM) tools have been developed and applied in order improve customer acquisition and retention, increase of portability and to support important analytical tasks such as predictive modeling and classification. Typically, CRM applications hold a huge set of information regarding each individual customer. This information is gained from customers' activity at the company, data entered by the customer in the process of registration, calls to support hotlines, etc. Proper analysis of this data can bring remarkable results for marketing purposes, but also for identifying customers which are likely to cancel their contract. Typically, database entries are scored using a statistical model defined over various attributes, which characterize the customers. These attributes are often called predictor variables. Higher scores reveal greater possibility of churning. Models are being built using statistical techniques like regression analysis, classification trees and neural networks.

4.2.1. Churn Prediction Methodology

For finding answers to the questions who and why is likely to churn a classification of the customers is needed. Churn prediction deals, therefore, with the identification of customers likely to churn in the near future. The basis for this is historical data, containing information about past churners. A comparison is made between these churners and existing customers. As likely churners are identified customers for which the classification suggests similarity to prior churners. Mitchell, (1997) summarizes different terms used for construction of a classification procedure as pattern recognition, discrimination or supervised learning.

Data Set Service providers can easily acquire huge volumes of data. Den Poel and Lariviere, (2004) presented four sets of data variables: customer behaviour, customer perceptions, customer demographics and macro environment variables. Customer behavior identifies which parts of the service a customer is using and how often is he using them. Interesting are product-specific ownership (which product/service is owned/on loan), total product ownership (number of products owned/on loan); inter purchase time (time between the purchase of two different articles). In telecommunications, for example, the provider can track number and length of calls, period between calls, the usage of the network for data exchange, etc. Customer perceptions are defined as the way a customer apprehends the service. They can be measured with customer surveys and include data like overall satisfaction, quality of service, problem experience, satisfaction with problem handling, pricing, location convenience, image/reputation of the company, customer perception of dependency to the vendor, etc.

Customer demographics are some of the most used variables for churn prediction. They include age, gender, level of education, social status, geographical data, etc. Macro environment variables identify changes in the world, different experiences of customers, which can affect the way they use a service. For example, in the telecommunication industry people who have survived a natural disaster and could rely on their mobile phones during it are more likely to continue using the service.

The size of gathered data is usually very large, which results in high dimensionality, make analyze a complex and challenging task. Therefore, before beginning to use a churn prediction method a data reduction technique is used, deciding with application domain knowledge which attributes can be of use and which can be ignored. Missing values should also be regarded - on attribute level these can be ignored if they are with low significance, whereas on record level they have to be replaced with a reasonable estimate, for example using interpolation. Providing a good estimate for this missing value is an important issue for proper churn prediction. The typical approach to the problem of churn prediction is using a sufficiently large data set that contains churning and non-churning customers. This set is being analyzed to construct a classifier. The work of a classifier is to decide, given a customer data set, if churn is more or less likely. Such classifiers are constructed using, for instance, neural networks, Bayesian statistics or decision trees constructed with the he heuristics like CART or C4.5 (Quinlan, 1993).

Table 4.1: Churn Prediction Categories

	Actual Churners	Actual Non Churners
Predicted Churners	True Positive	False Positive
Predicted Churners	Non False Negative	True Negative

Quality of the output is then measured in terms of sensitivity, specificity and accuracy. Table 1 shows the categorization of churn prediction. The sensitivity of a classifier is the number of data sets for which correct predictions have been made (true positives, in our case: churners predicted as churners) divided by the total number of members (true positives +false positives). The specificity is the number of data sets that were correctly predicted to not be members of the class (true negatives, non churners predicted as non churners) divided by the number of all members that do not belong to the class. Usually a Receiver Operating Characteristic (ROC) curve is used to display a graphic of sensitivity vs. specificity. Accuracy is defined as the percentage of correct predictions. This quality measures are used to adjust parameters of the classifier until a reasonable quality of prediction is achieved. According to Domingos, (1999) accuracy of about 90% is sufficient for a classifier to predict churning.

Regression is considered to be a good technique for identifying and predicting customer satisfaction. For each of the variables in a regression model the standard error rate is calculated using SPSS. Then the variables with the most significance in respect to linear regressions for churn prediction are obtained and a regression model is constructed. Since the prediction task in churn prognosis is to identify a customer as a churner or non churner and therefore the prediction attribute is associated with only two values logistic regression techniques are suitable. While linear regression models are useful for prediction of continuous valued attributes, logistic regression models are suitable for binary attributes. The logistic regression model is simply a non-linear transformation of a liner regression model. The standard representation of logistic regression is referred as logit function. The estimated probability of churn is estimated with the function

$$P_r[churn] = \frac{1}{1 + e^{-T}}$$

where T = a + BX. Here a is a constant term, X represents the predictor attributes vector and B is the coefficient vector for the predictor attributes. If T equals 0 the probability is 0, 5. This means that it is equip-probable that a customer is a churner and non churner. With T growing large the probability comes closer to 1, so the customer becomes a more probable churner, when T is becoming small the probability of churn is tending to be 0. Naive Bayes is a type of supervised-learning module that contains examples of the input-target mapping the model tries to learn. Such models make predictions about new data based on the examination of previous data. The Naïve Bayes algorithm uses the mathematics of Bayes' Theorem to make its predictions.

$$P_r[A|B] = \frac{P_r(B|A)P_r(A)}{P_r(B)}$$

Bayes Theorem (2) states that the probability of a particular predicted event, given the evidence in this instance, is computed from three other numbers: the probability of that prediction in similar situations in general, ignoring the specific evidence (the so called prior probability) multiplied with the probability of seeing the evidence there they have, given that the particular prediction is correct divided by the probability of that prediction in general.

Decision Trees are the most commonly used tool for predictions and classification of future events. The developments of such trees are done in two major steps: building and pruning. During the first phase the data set is partitioned recursively until most of the records in each partition contain identical value. The second phase then removes some branches which contain noisy data (those with the largest estimated error rate). CART, a Classification and Regression Tree, is constructed by recursive splits of an instance into subgroups until a specified criterion has been met. The tree grows until the decrease of impurity falls below a user-defined threshold. Each node in a Decision Tree is a test condition and the branching is based on the value of the attribute being tested. The tree is representing a collection of multiple rule sets. When evaluating a customer data set the classification is done by traversing through the tree until a leaf node is reached. The label of this leaf node (Churner or Non Churner) is assigned to the customer record under evaluation. Decision Trees are often criticized that they are not suitable for capturing complex and non-linear relationships between the attributes. Nevertheless, research shows (Hadden et al., 2006a, Hadden et al., 2006b, Quinlan, 1993) that the accuracy of decision trees and training data requirements are high.

The use of neural networks in churn prediction has a big asset in respect of other methods used because the likelihood of each classification made can also be determined that neural networks outperform decision trees for prediction of churn (Au et al., 2003). They state the biggest disadvantage of neural networks – they do not uncover patterns in an easily understandable form, categorizing them as a 'black box' model. The basic idea behind neural networks is that each attribute is associated with a weight and combinations of weighted attributes participate in the prediction task. During learning the weights are constantly updated, thus correcting the 'effect' which an attribute has. Given a customer data set and the set of predictor variables the neural network tries to calculate a combination of the inputs and to output the probability that the customer is a churner. Accuracy achieved by neural networks fully outweighs the disadvantage that they need a large volume of data set and a lot of time in order to calculate a reasonable weightage for the predictor attributes. Iwata et al., (2006) proved that neural networks are superior in performance as opposed to other models. Similar results were identified in (Hadden et al., 2006a, Hadden et al., 2006b).

4.2.2. *Problems in Churn Prediction*

Although conventional churn prediction techniques have the advantage of being simple and robust, it defects in the input data, they posse's serious limitations to the interpretation of reasons for churn. A proper insight on the reasons for churning is essential in order to design effective retention methods. Therefore, measuring the effectiveness of a prediction model depends also on how well the results can be interpreted for inferring the possible reasons of churn. This is done in order to properly allocate limited time and resources for retention efforts by choosing more probable churners with the help of successful (in previous efforts for the given reason) techniques. Neural networks, being best in terms of performance have proven to be best for actual churn prediction. The results can then be further analyzed using linear regression and decision trees for explaining the behavior of churn.

In Evolutionary Approach The necessity of precise interpretation of churn prediction results motivated for researchers to give suggestion of new and precise models, which not only offer insights whether a customer is likely to churn or not, but also focus on reasons for churning. An evolutionary algorithm learning of rules for churn has been proposed (Au et al., 2003). The algorithm is described by the authors as follows: The evolutionary process begins with the generation of an initial set of first-order rules (i.e., rules with one conjunct/condition) using a probabilistic induction technique and based on these rules, rules of higher order (two or more conjuncts) are obtained iteratively.

1. When identifying interesting rules, an objective interestingness measure is used.
2. The fitness of a chromosome is defined in terms of the probability that the attribute values of a record can be correctly determined using the rules it encodes and
3. The likelihood of predictions (or classifications) made are estimated so that subscribers can be ranked according to their likelihood to churn.

Ultsch, (1999) Self-organizing Maps described how a combination of emergent self organizing maps. U-Matrix methods and knowledge conversion can be used for churn prediction and conversion, creating an effective churn prediction classifier. In this approach groups amongst customers are identified. Group characteristics are being summarized using rules. Research results have shown a correct prediction of 90%. The main idea is that identification of groups and their characteristics can lead to better understanding of the real reasons for churning.

4.2.3. Customer Lifetime Value

Once churners have been identified and reasons for quitting have been found rapid action has to be taken by the marketing department in order to prevent churn properly. Usually the time is not enough to address all likely churners. Therefore, further decision making has to be done to choose the clients that will be contacted. For the customers with highest probability of churning it is predicted how much revenue a service provider is going to get over the period of customers' stay. In this way valuable customers are identified and efforts are made of retaining these customers. An inversely proportional rate of customer lifetime value of an existing customer to the churn probability of that customer can be seen (Rosset et al., 2002), but the customers' decision to stay back is usually coupled with increment of lifetime value of that customer. Using customer lifetime value in addition to churn prediction can minimize the cost for making a needless retention effort (false positives) and the cost of losing a customer because the model did not predict he is likely to churn (false negatives).

4.3. Class Imbalance

The common understanding about class imbalance in the literature is concerned with the situation in which some classes of data are highly under-represented compared to other classes (He and Garcia, 2009). By convention, the under-represented class is called the minority class, and correspondingly the class having the larger size is called the majority class. Misclassifying is an example from the minority class is usually more costly. For SDP, due to the nature of the problem, the defect case is much less likely to happen than the non-defect case. The defect class is thus the minority. The recognition of this class is more important, because the failure of finding a defect could degrade software quality greatly.

The challenge of learning from imbalanced data is that the relatively or absolutely underrepresented class cannot draw equal attention to the learning algorithm compared to the majority class, which often leads to very specific classification rules or missing rules for the minority class without much generalization ability for future prediction (Weiss, 2004). The learning objective can be generally described as "obtaining a classifier that will provide high accuracy for the minority class without severely jeopardizing the accuracy of the majority class" (He and Garcia, 2009).

Numerous methods have been proposed to tackle class imbalance problems at data and algorithm levels. Data-level methods include a variety of re-sampling techniques, manipulating training data to rectify the skewed class distributions, such as random oversampling, random under sampling, and SMOTE (Chawla et al., 2002). They are simple and efficient, but their effectiveness depends greatly on the problem and training algorithms (Estabrooks et al., 2004). Algorithm-level methods address class imbalance by modifying their training mechanism directly with the goal of better accuracy on the minority class, including one-class learning (Japkowicz et al., 1995), and cost-sensitive learning algorithms (He and Garcia, 2009, Zhou and Liu et al., 2006). Algorithm-level methods require specific treatments for different kinds of learning algorithms, which hinders their use in many applications; because they do not know in advance which algorithm would be the best choice in most cases.

In addition to the aforementioned data-level and algorithm-level solutions, ensemble learning (HoT et al., 1994, Rokach, 2010) has become another major category of approaches to handling imbalanced data by combining multiple classifiers, such as SMOTEBoost, and AdaBoost.NC (Wang and Yao, 2012). Ensemble learning algorithms have been shown to be able to combine strength from individual learners, and enhance the overall performance (Brown et al., 2005, Tang, 2006). They also offer additional opportunities to handle class imbalance at both the individual and ensemble levels. The under sampling strategies are shown in, and two ensemble methods (Wang and Yao, 2012) because of their simplicity, effectiveness, and popularity in the literature. Threshold-moving is also considered in this study as a frequently used cost-sensitive technique (Zhou and Liu et al., 2006).

4.3.1. *Multiclass Imbalance*

Most existing solutions for multiclass imbalance problems use class decomposition schemes to handle multiclass and work with two-class imbalance techniques to handle each imbalanced binary subtask. For example, protein fold classification is a typical multiclass imbalance problem. (Rifkin and Klautau, 2004, Hastie and Tibshirani, 1998) schemes to break down this problem and then built rule-based learners to improve the coverage of minority class examples. OAA and OAO are two most popular schemes of class decomposition in the literature. OAA are used to handle multiclass and undersampling and SMOTE (Chawla et al., 2002) techniques to overcome the imbalance issue. It was investigated that a variety of oversampling and undersampling techniques used with OAA for a weld flaw classification problem. Algorithm uses OAA to deal with multiclass and then applied some advanced sampling methods that decompose each binary problem further so as to rebalance the data.

Fernandez et al., (2010) integrated OAO and SMOTE in their algorithm. Instead of applying data level methods, Algorithm proposed by Alejo et al., (2009) made the error function of neural networks cost sensitive by incorporating the imbalance rates between classes to emphasize minority classes, after decomposing the problem through OAA. Generally speaking, class decomposition simplifies the problem. However, each individual classifier is trained without full data knowledge. It can cause classification ambiguity or uncovered data regions with respect to each type of decomposition.

Different from the previous discussion, a cost-sensitive ensemble algorithm was proposed (Sun, 2006), which addresses multiclass imbalance directly without using class decomposition. Its key focuses are how to find an appropriate cost matrix with multiple classes and how to introduce the costs into the algorithm. A genetic algorithm (GA) was applied to search for the optimum cost setup of each class. Two kinds of fitness were tested, G-mean (Kubat, 1997) and F-measure (Rijsbergen, 1979), the most frequently used measures for performance evaluation in class imbalance learning. The choice depends on the training objective. The obtained cost vector was then integrated into a cost-sensitive version of AdaBoost. M1 (Freund and Schapire, 1997), namely, AdaC2 (Sun et al., 2005, Sun et al., 2007), is able to process multiclass data sets. However, searching the best cost vector is very time consuming due to the nature of GA. No existing methods can deal with multiclass imbalance problems efficiently and effectively yet to our best knowledge.

Single-class performance measures evaluate how well a classifier performs in one class, particularly the minority class. Recall, precision, and F-measure (Rijsbergen, 1979) are widely discussed single-class measures for two-class problems, which are still applicable to multiclass problems. Recall is a measure of completeness; precision is a measure of exactness. F-measure incorporates both to express their tradeoff. For the overall performance, G-mean (Kubat, 1997) and AUC (Bradley, 1997) are often used in the literature, but they are originally designed for two class problems. Therefore, they have to be adapted to multiclass scenarios: an extended G-mean (Sun, 2006) is defined as the geometric mean of recall values of all classes; a commonly accepted extension of AUC is called M measure or MAUC (Hand and Till, 2001), the average AUC of all pairs of classes.

4.3.2. Boosting Algorithms in Imbalance

NC combines the strength of negative correlation learning and boosting. It emphasizes ensemble diversity explicitly during training and shows very encouraging empirical results in both effectiveness and efficiency in comparison with the conventional AdaBoost and other NCL methods in general cases. It got exploited that it is good generalization performance to facilitate class imbalance learning, based on the finding that ensemble diversity has a positive role in solving this type of problem.

Comprehensive experiments were carried out on a set of two-class imbalance problems. The results suggest that AdaBoost. NC combined with random oversampling can improve the prediction accuracy on the minority class without losing the overall performance compared to other existing class imbalance learning methods. It is achieved by providing less overfitting and broader classification boundaries for the minority class. Applying oversampling is simply to maintain a sufficient number of minority class examples and to guarantee that two classes receive equal attention from the algorithm. AdaBoost. NC penalizes classification errors and encourages ensemble diversity sequentially with the AdaBoost training framework. Much research has been performed with respect to the class imbalance problem. Weiss, (2004) provides a survey of the class imbalance problem and techniques for reducing the negative impact imbalance that has on classification performance. The study identifies many methods for alleviating the problem of class imbalance, including data sampling and boosting, which are the two techniques investigated.

Japkowicz et al, (2000) presents another study addressing the issue of class imbalance, including an investigation of the types of imbalance that most negatively impact classification performance, and a small case study comparing several techniques for alleviating the problem. Data sampling has received much attention in research related to class imbalance. Data sampling attempts to overcome imbalanced class distributions by adding examples to (oversampling) or removing examples from (under sampling) the data set. The simplest form of under sampling is Random Under Sampling (RUS). RUS randomly removes examples from the majority class until a desired class distribution is found. While there is no universally accepted optimal class distribution, a balanced (50:50) distribution is often considered to be near optimal (Weiss and Provost, 2003). However, when examples from the minority class are very rare, a ratio closer to 35:65 (minority: majority) may result in better classification performance (Khoshgoftaar et al., 2007).

In addition to random data sampling techniques, several more "intelligent" algorithms for re-sampling data have been proposed. Barandela et al, (2004) and Han et al, (2005) examine the performance of some of these "intelligent" data sampling techniques, such as SMOTE, borderline SMOTE, and Wilson's editing. Van Hulse et al, (2007) examined the performance of seven different data sampling techniques (both "intelligent" and random) using a large number of different learning algorithms and experimental data sets, finding both RUS and SMOTE to be very effective data sampling techniques. Another technique for dealing with class imbalance is boosting. While boosting is not specifically designed to handle the class imbalance problem, it has been shown to be very effective in this regard (Seiffert and Khoshgoftaar, 2008).

The most commonly used boosting algorithm is AdaBoost (Freund and R. Schapire, 1996), which has been shown to improve the performance of any weak classifier, provided that the classifier results in better performance than random guessing. Several variations have been proposed to make AdaBoost cost sensitive (Fan et al, 1999, Ting, 2000, Sun et al, 2007) or to improve its performance on imbalanced data (Joshi et al., 2001, Guo and Viktor, 2004, Mease et al., 2007). One of the most promising of these techniques is SMOTEBoost (Chawla et al., 2003). SMOTEBoost combines an intelligent oversampling technique (SMOTE) with AdaBoost, resulting in a highly effective hybrid approach to learning from imbalanced data. Boosting is a meta learning technique designed to improve the classification performance of weak learners by iteratively creating an ensemble of weak hypotheses which are combined to predict the class of unlabeled examples. AdaBoost, which is a well-known boosting algorithm shown to improve the classification performance of weak classifiers. We present a brief synopsis of AdaBoost.

During the iteration of AdaBoost, a weak hypothesis is formed by the base learner. The error associated with the hypothesis is calculated, and the weight of each example is adjusted such that misclassified examples have their weights increased while correctly classified examples have their weights decreased. Therefore, subsequent iterations of boosting will generate hypotheses that are more likely to correctly classify the previously mislabeled examples. After all iterations are completed, a weighted vote of all hypotheses is used to assign a class to the unlabeled examples. All boosting algorithms (AdaBoost, SMOTEBoost, and RUSBoost) are performed using ten iterations. Preliminary experiments with AdaBoost using the same data sets showed no significant improvement between 10 and 50 iterations. Since boosting assigns higher weights to misclassified examples and minority class examples are those most likely to be misclassified, it stands to reason that minority class examples will receive higher weights during the boosting process, making it similar in many ways to cost-sensitive classification (Elkan, 2001). In effect, boosting alters the distribution of the training data (through weighting, not altering the number of examples); thus, it can also be thought of as an advanced data sampling technique (Weiss and Provost, 2003). For simplicity, they refer to boosting as one of the five "sampling techniques".

Data sampling techniques attempt to alleviate the problem of class imbalance by adjusting the class distribution of the training data set. This can be accomplished by either removing examples from the majority class (under sampling) or adding examples to the minority class (oversampling). One of the most common data sampling techniques (largely due to its simplicity) is RUS. Unlike more complex data sampling algorithms, RUS makes no attempt to "intelligently" remove examples from the training data.

Instead, RUS simply removes examples from the majority class at random until a desired class distribution is achieved. In their paper, they used three post sampling class distributions: 35, 50, and 65. These numbers represent the percentage of examples in the post sampling data set, which belong to the minority class. The same three values are used when performing SMOTE, SMOTEBoost, and RUSBoost.

Chawla et al, (2002) proposed an intelligent oversampling method called SMOTE. SMOTE adds new artificial minority examples by extrapolating between preexisting minority instances rather than simply duplicating original examples. The newly created instances because the minority regions of the feature space to be fuller and more general. The technique first finds the k nearest neighbors of each minority example where the paper recommends k = 5. The artificial examples are then generated in the direction of some or all of the nearest neighbors, depending on the amount of oversampling desired. If 200% oversampling is specified, then synthetic examples are generated randomly along the line segments connecting each minority example to two of its five nearest neighbors. If x_i is the minority example being examined, x_j is one of the selected nearest neighbors of xi, and xn is the new example being added to the data set, then $x_n = u(x_j - x_i) + x_i$, where u is a uniform random number between zero and one. This sampling process causes a classifier to learn a larger and more general decision region in the feature space, ideally alleviating the problem caused by class imbalance.

SMOTEBoost, which was proposed by Chawla et al, (2003) combines the SMOTE algorithm with AdaBoost, resulting in a hybrid sampling/boosting algorithm that outperforms both SMOTE and AdaBoost. As is the case with RUSBoost, SMOTEBoost is based on the AdaBoost.M2 algorithm. Prior to constructing the weak hypothesis during each round of boosting, SMOTE is applied to the training data to achieve a more balanced training data set. Therefore, the algorithm for SMOTEBoost is very similar to that of RUSBoost. The application of SMOTE at this point has two drawbacks that RUSBoost is designed to overcome. First, it increases the complexity of the algorithm. SMOTE must find the k nearest neighbors of the minority class examples and extrapolate between them to make new examples. RUS, on the other hand, simply deletes the majority class examples at random. Second, since SMOTE is an oversampling technique, it results in longer model training times. This effect is compounded by SMOTEBoost's use of boosting, since many models must be built using larger training data sets. On the other hand, RUS results in smaller training data sets and, therefore, shorter model training times.

4.4.   Class-Imbalanced Data Sets

The overwhelming amount of data that is currently available in any field of research poses new problems for data mining and knowledge discovery methods. The large amount of data makes most existing algorithms inapplicable to many real-world problems. Furthermore, one of the distinctive features of many common problems in data mining applications is the uneven distribution of the instances of the different classes. In extremely active research areas, such as artificial intelligence in medicine, bioinformatics, or intrusion detection, two classes are usually involved: a class of interest or a positive class, and a negative class that is overrepresented in the data sets. This is usually referred to as the class-imbalance problem (He and Garcia., 2009). In highly imbalanced problems, the ratio between the positive and negative classes can be as high as 1:1000 or 1:10000. It has been repeatedly shown that most classification methods suffer from an imbalanced distribution of training instances among classes (Chawla et al., 2002).

Most learning algorithms expect an approximately even distribution of instances among the different classes and suffer, to different degrees, when that is not the case. Dealing with the class-imbalance problem is a difficult but relevant task as many of the most interesting and challenging real-world problems have a very uneven class distribution. Many algorithms and methods have been proposed to ameliorate the effect of class imbalance on the performance of learning algorithms. There are two main approaches to these methods. Internal approaches acting on the algorithm approaches modify the learning algorithm to deal with the imbalance problem. They can adapt the decision threshold to create a bias toward the minority class or introduce costs in the learning process to compensate the minority class. External approaches acting on the data algorithms act on the data instead of the learning method. They have the advantage of being independent from the classifier used. There are two basic approaches: Over sampling the minority class and Under sampling the majority class. Combined approaches are based on boosting accounting for the imbalance in the training set. These methods modify the basic boosting method to account for minority class underrepresentation in the data set.

There are two principal advantages of choosing sampling over cost-sensitive methods. First, sampling is more general as it does not depend on the possibility of adapting a certain algorithm to work with classification costs. Second, the learning algorithm is not modified, which can cause difficulties and add additional parameters to be tuned. Data-driven algorithms can be broadly classified into two groups: those that under sample the majority class and those that oversample the minority class. There are also algorithms that combine both processes. Both under sampling and oversampling can be randomly achieved or through a more complicated process of searching for least or most useful instances. Under sampling the majority class usually leads to better results than oversampling the minority class when oversampling is performed using sampling with replacement from the minority class.

Furthermore, combining under sampling of the majority class with oversampling of the minority class has not yielded better results than under sampling of the majority class alone (Ling and Li, 1998). One of the possible sources of the problematic performance of oversampling is the fact that no new information is introduced in the training set as oversampling must rely on adding new copies of minority class instances already in the data set. Sampling has proven a very efficient method of dealing with class-imbalanced data sets (Weiss and Provost, 2001, Estabrooks et al., 2004). Removing instances only from the majority class, usually referred to as One-Sided Selection (OSS) (Kubat and Matwin, 1997), has two major problems. First, reduction is limited by the number of instances of the minority class. Second, instances from the minority class are never removed, even when their contribution to the model's performance is harmful.

However, few attempts have been made to cope with class imbalanced data sets using instance selection algorithms, which can remove instances from both the minority and majority classes. Standard widely used methods can be applied, but they do not achieve good results because their design bias is not focused on these kinds of problems. Evolutionary computation has been used with more success (Garcia et al., 2012), but scalability is important (Garcia Pedrajas et al., 2010), and those methods cannot be applied to large and very large data sets. The method discussed in (Garcia Pedrajas et al., 2010) has two major objectives:

Improving the performance of previous approaches based of instances selection for class-imbalanced data sets and developing a method that is able to scale up to very large, and even huge, problems. The class-imbalanced nature of the problem is dealt with by means of two mechanisms. First, the selection of instances from the majority and minority classes is performed separately. Second, selection is driven by a fitness function that takes accuracy in both classes into account. Furthermore, at its inner level, all the selection process is always performed in balanced sets. The divide-and-conquer philosophy (Garcia Pedrajas et al., 2010) addresses the problem of scalability without compromising its performance. The method is based on applying an instance selection algorithm to balanced subsets of the whole training set and on combining the results obtained from those subsets by means of a voting scheme. As an additional and very useful feature, the method has linear time complexity and can be easily implemented in a shared or distributed memory parallel machine. When dealing with class-imbalanced data sets, the main aim is improving accuracy. However, if a method achieves the same accuracy using fewer instances, that method would be preferable. Moreover, many of the most relevant class-imbalanced problems appear in very large data sets where data reduction is a must.

4.5.   Summary

This chapter provided the churn predication introduction, types of churn, general methodology of churn prediction, problems in churn prediction, value of the customer lifetime, class imbalance, multiclass imbalance, boosting algorithms in imbalance. The next chapter discusses proposed work.

CHAPTER 5

DESIGN OF MODIFIED RIPPER ALGORITHM

5.1. Introduction

This chapter discusses on various algorithms towards customer churn prediction. The Banks usually make a distinction between voluntary churn and involuntary churn. Voluntary churn occurs due to a decision by the customer to switch to another bank, involuntary churn occurs due to circumstances such as a customer's relocation to a long-term care facility, death, or the relocation to a distant location. In most applications, involuntary reasons for churn are excluded from the analytical models. Analysts tend to concentrate on voluntary churn, because it typically occurs through bank-customer relationship which is controlled by bank, such as transaction interactions, services offered etc. The existing algorithms such as Decision Tree, Weighted Random Forest and Gradient Boosting Algorithm are depicted in this chapter. The proposed mechanism for customer churn prediction makes use of Genetic Algorithm, k-Nearest Neighbor and Ripper. A new algorithm has been proposed namely Modified Ripper Algorithm. The next section depicts the framework of the research design.

5.2. Evaluation Metrics

The six categories of problems are associated while mining imbalanced classes. They are improper evaluation metrics, lack of data, relative lack of data, data fragmentation, inappropriate inductive bias and noise. To solve these issues, the present work considers, improper evaluation metrics, sampling, learn only the rare classes, non-greedy search techniques and more appropriate inductive bias.

Improper Evaluation Metrics

It was often hard or nearly impossible to construct a perfect classification model that would correctly classify all examples from the test set. Therefore, a suboptimal classification model that best suits the needs and works best on the problem of churn prediction of credit card holder to be selected. Churn prediction, in this study, is treated as a two-class classification problem (binary prediction), where a class is either positive (card holder is a churner) or negative (card holder is a non-churner). The classification metrics, specificity, sensitivity, Yrate, precision, accuracy and misclassification error are used for analyzing the proposed predictors. Along with this Area Under Curve (AUC) is also used.

Cost-Sensitive Learning

During churn prediction, the rare cases are of primary interest, where the metrics alone would not suffice. An alternative solution to these situations is cost-sensitive learning methods (Weiss, 2004), which exploits facts that the value of correctly identifying the positive (rare) class outweights the value of correctly identifying the common class. For two-class problems, this is done by associating greater cost with false negatives than with false positives. Assigning a greater cost of false negatives than to false positives improves performance with respect to the positive (rare) class.

Sampling

Sampling is the most used technique to handle rare cases and classes. Here, the basic idea is to eliminate or minimize rarity by altering the distribution of training examples. Four types of sampling methods are used in the study. They are Under-Sampling, Over-Sampling, Boosting and CUBE, an Advanced Under Sampling method. Under-Sampling eliminates majority-class examples while Over-Sampling, in its simplest form, duplicates minority class examples. Both of these sampling techniques decrease the overall level of class imbalance, thereby making the rare class less rare. Boosting is a technique for improving the accuracy of a predictive function by applying the function repeatedly in a series and combining the output of each function with weighting so that the total error of the prediction is minimized.

Learn Only the Rare Classes

When learning a set of classification rule for all classes, it is found that several rare classes are ignored and hence, the only solution is to predict rare classes. This technique is proven using Support Vector Machines and Neural Networks and one data mining technique that utilizes this recognition-based approach is a Hippo. Ripper is a rule induction system that utilizes a separate-and-conquer approach to iteratively build rules to cover previously uncovered training examples. Each rule is grown by adding conditions until no negative examples are covered. It normally generates rules for each class from the most 'rare class' to the most 'common class'. Given this architecture, it is quite straightforward to learn rules only for the minority class, a capability that Ripper provides. The ripper method is enhanced in this research by including a swapping operation for easy prediction of churn and non-churn cases and a partitioning method are included to split the dataset for easy analysis.

Non-Greedy Search Technique

Genetic algorithm, a non-greedy technique, is proposed to handle imbalance classes. The technique makes use of candidate solution instead of single solution and then employs stochastic operators. It gives a conclusion that genetic algorithms work better with attribute interaction and thus avoids getting stuck into local maxima, which all together makes genetic algorithms suitable finding rarity. This would give a clear idea that for what reason genetic algorithms are being increasingly used for data mining. Several systems have relied on the power of genetic algorithms to handle rarity. Some of them used a genetic algorithm to predict very rare events while and other researchers tried to use a genetic algorithm to discover, small disjunct rules (Weiss, 1999).

More Appropriate Inductive Bias

Several attempts have been taken to improve the performance of data mining systems with respect to rarity by choosing a more appropriate bias. The simplest approach involves modifying existing systems to eliminate some small disjuncts based on tests of statistical significance or using error estimation techniques. The hope is that this will remove only improperly learned disjuncts (Weiss, 1995). Unfortunately, this approach was shown not only to degrade performance with respect to rarity, but also to degrade overall classification performance. This study, proposes the use of the decision tree algorithm, namely, C4.5. The following table (Table5.1) summarizes the data mining problem and the mapped solution to each problem as proposed in this study.

Table 5.1: Data Mining Problems Mapped to its Solutions to Address these Problems

Data Mining Problem	Method Mapped to Address the problem
Improper Evaluation Metrics	More appropriate evaluation Metrics Cost-sensitive learning
Absolute Rarity	Learn only the rare class Sampling (over- and under) Cost-sensitive learning More appropriate evaluation metrics
Relative Rarity	More appropriate inductive bias Boosting
Data fragmentation	Non-greedy search techniques Learn only the rare class Sampling (over- and under)
Inappropriate bias	More appropriate inductive bias Appropriate evaluation metrics Cost-sensitive learning
Noise	Advanced sampling More appropriate inductive bias

5.3. Framework

The proposed research work aims in design and development of customer churn prediction in banking sector. The framework is developed to extract and classify the churners among the customers through class imbalance. The proposed work uses mechanisms namely Decision Tree (DT), Gradient Boosting (GB), Weighted Random Forest (WRF), Genetic Algorithm (GA), k-Nearest Neighbor (k-NN) and Ripper Algorithm (RA). It also demonstrates three sampling methods namely Random Over Sampling, Random Under Sampling and Advanced Random Under

Sampling with experimental results and discussions. A new algorithm has been proposed as Modified Ripper Algorithm (MRA). Evaluation techniques such as Area Under Curve (AUC), Error and Accuracy are used. By using these entire techniques class imbalance is predicted. All these concepts are clearly defined in the following figure 5.1.

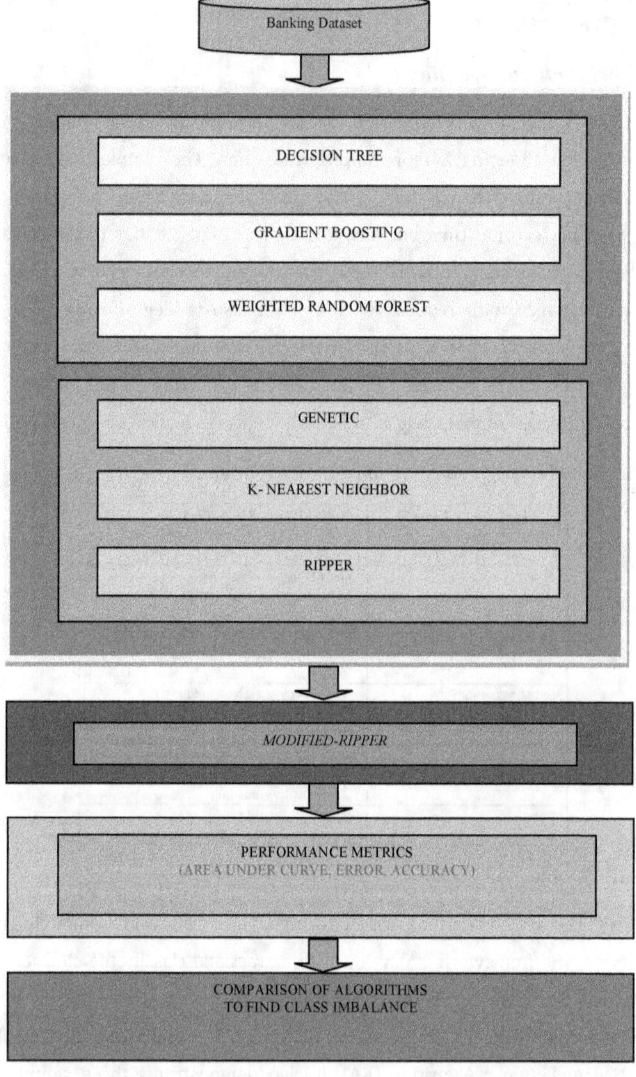

Figure 5.1: Framework

5.4. Classification Algorithms

5.4.1. Decision Tree

A decision tree is a classifier expressed as a recursive partition of the instance space. The decision tree consists of nodes that form a rooted tree, meaning it is a directed tree with a node called "root" that has no incoming edges. All other nodes have exactly one incoming edge. A node with outgoing edges is called an internal or test node. All other nodes are called leaves (also known as terminal or decision nodes). In a decision tree, each internal node splits the instance space into two or more sub-spaces according to a certain discrete function of the input attributes values.

In the simplest and most frequent case, each test considers a single attribute, such that the instance space is partitioned according to the attribute's value. In the case of numeric attributes, the condition refers to a range. Each leaf is assigned to one class representing the most appropriate target value. Alternatively, the leaf may hold a probability vector indicating the probability of the target attribute having a certain value. Instances are classified by navigating them from the root of the tree down to a leaf, according to the outcome of the tests along the path. Fig 5.2 describes a decision tree that reasons whether or not a potential customer will respond to a direct mailing.

Internal nodes are represented as circles, whereas leaves are denoted as triangles. Note that this decision tree incorporates both nominal and numeric attributes. Given this classifier, the analyst can predict the response of a potential customer (by sorting it down the tree), and understand the behavioral characteristics of the entire potential customers population regarding direct mailing. Each node is labeled with the attribute it tests, and its branches are labeled with its corresponding values. In case of numeric attributes, decision trees can be geometrically interpreted as a collection of hyper-planes, each orthogonal to one of the axes. Naturally, decision-makers prefer less complex decision trees, since they may be considered more comprehensible.

Furthermore, according to Breiman et al., (1984) the tree complexity has a crucial effect on its accuracy. The tree complexity is explicitly controlled by the stopping criteria used and the pruning method employed. Usually the tree complexity is measured by one of the following metrics: the total number of nodes, total number of leaves, tree depth and number of attributes used. Decision tree induction is closely related to rule induction.

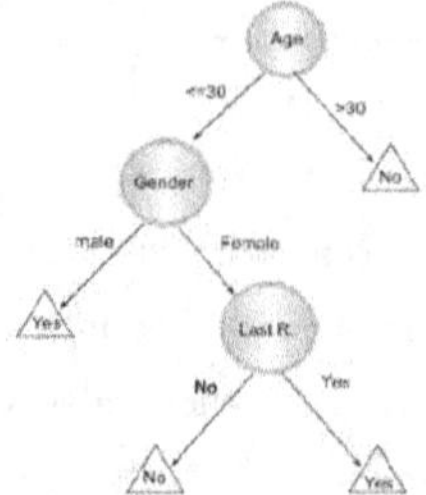

Figure 5.2: Decision Tree

<u>TreeGrowing (S,A,y)</u>
Where:
S - Training Set
A - Input Feature Set
y - Target Feature
Create a new tree T with a single root node.
IF One of the Stopping Criteria is fulfilled THEN
        Mark the root node in T as a leaf with the most
        common value of y in S as a label.
ELSE
Find a discrete function f(A) of the input
        attributes values such that splitting S
        according to f(A)'s outcomes (v1,...,vn) gains
        the best splitting metric.
IF best splitting metric > treshold THEN
        Label t with f(A)
        FOR each outcome vi of f(A):

                Set Subtree$_i$= TreeGrowing ($\sigma_{f(A)=vi}$S,A,y).
                Connect the root node of tT to Subtreei with
                    an edge that is labelled as v$_i$
        END FOR
ELSE
        Mark the root node in T as a leaf with the most
            Common value of y in S as a label.
        END IF
END IF
RETURN T
<u>TreePruning (S,T,y)</u>
Where:
        S - Training Set
        y - Target Feature
        T - The tree to be pruned
DO
        Select a node t in T such that pruning it
            maximally improve some evaluation criteria
IF t$\neq$Ø THEN T=pruned(T,t)
UNTIL t=Ø
RETURN T

Figure 5.3: Decision Tree Algorithm

Each path from the root of a decision tree to one of its leaves can be transformed into a rule simply by conjoining the tests along the path to form the antecedent part, and taking the leaf's class prediction as the class value. The resulting rule set can then be simplified to improve its comprehensibility to a human user, and possibly its accuracy (Quinlan, 1987). Decision tree inducers are algorithms that automatically construct a decision tree from a given dataset. Typically the goal is to find the optimal decision tree by minimizing the generalization error. However, other target functions can be also defined, for instance, minimizing the number of nodes or minimizing the average depth. Induction of an optimal decision tree from a given data is considered to be a hard task. It has been shown that finding a minimal decision tree consistent with the training set is NP–hard (Hancock et al., 1996).

Moreover, it has been shown that constructing a minimal binary tree with respect to the expected number of tests required for classifying an unseen instance is NP–complete (Hyafil and Rivest, 1976). Even finding the minimal equivalent decision tree for a given decision tree (Zantema and Bodlaender, 2000) or building the optimal decision tree from decision tables is known to be NP–hard (Naumov, 1991). The results will indicate that using optimal decision tree algorithms is feasible only in small problems. Consequently, heuristics methods are required for solving the problem. Roughly speaking, these methods can be divided into two groups: top–down and bottom–up with clear preference in the literature to the first group which is explained clearly in Fig 5.3.

5.4.2. *Weighted Random Forest*

Weighted Random Forests are an ensemble learning method for classification (and regression) that operate by constructing a multitude of decision trees at training time and outputting the class that is the mode of the classes output by individual trees. The algorithm for inducing a random forest was developed by Breiman et al., (1984) and "Random Forests" is their trademark. The term came from random decision forests that were first proposed by Tin Kam Ho of Bell Labs, (1995). The method combines Breiman's "bagging" idea and the random selection of features, introduced independently by them in order to construct a collection of decision trees with controlled variance. The selection of a random subset of features is an example of the random subspace method, which, in Ho's formulation, is a way to implement classification proposed by Kleinberg, (1996).

The early development of random forests introduced the idea of searching over a random subset of the available decisions when splitting a node, in the context of growing a single tree as explained in figure 5.4. The idea of random subspace selection from Ho and Tin Kam, (1995) was also influential in the design of random forests. In this method a forest of trees is grown, and variation among the trees is introduced by projecting the training data into a randomly chosen subspace before fitting each tree. Finally, the idea of randomized node optimization is explained where the decision at each node is selected by a randomized procedure, rather than a deterministic optimization.

```
Require: Initially the tree has exactly one leaf (TreeRoot) which covers the whole space
Require: The dimensionality of the input, D. Parameters λ, m and τ.
    SelectCandidateSplitDimensions(TreeRoot, min(1 + Poisson(λ); D))
    for t = 1::: do
        Receive (Xt; Yt; It) from the environment
        At ←leaf containing Xt
        if It = estimation then
            UpdateEstimationStatistics(At, (Xt; Yt))
            for all S ∈ CandidateSplits(At) do
                for all A ∈ CandidateChildren(S) do
                    if Xt ∈ A then
                        UpdateEstimationStatistics(A, (Xt; Yt))
                    end if
                end for
            end for
        else if It = structure then
            if At has fewer than m candidate split points then
                for all d ∈ CandidateSplitDimensions(At) do
                    CreateCandidateSplit(At, d; πd Xt)
                end for
            end if
            for all S ∈ CandidateSplits(At) do
                for all A ∈ CandidateChildren(S) do
                    if Xt ∈ A then
                        UpdateStructuralStatistics(A, (Xt; Yt))
                    end if
                end for
            end for
            if CanSplit(At) then
                if ShouldSplit(At) then
                    Split(At)
                Else if MustSplit(At) then
                    Split(At)
                end if
            end if
        end if
    end for
```

Figure 5.4: Weighted Random Forest Algorithm

The introduction of random forests proper was first made in a paper by Leo Breiman, (1984) that describes a method of building a forest of uncorrelated trees using a CART like procedure, combined with randomized node optimization and bagging. In addition, it combines several ingredients, some previously known and some novel, which form the basis of the modern practice of random forests, in particular: Using out-of-bag error as an estimate of the generalization error, Measuring variable importance through permutation. It also offers the first theoretical result for weighted random forests in the form of a bound on the generalization error and weights that depends on the strength of the trees in the forest and their correlation.

5.4.3. *Gradient Boosting*

Gradient Boosting is a machine learning technique for regression problems, which produces a prediction model in the form of an ensemble of weak prediction models, typically Decision Trees. It builds the model in a stage-wise fashion like other boosting methods do, and it generalizes them by allowing optimization of an arbitrary differentiable loss function. The Gradient Boosting method can also be used for classification problems by reducing them to regression with a suitable loss function. The method was invented and published in a series of two papers, the first of which introduced the method, and the second one described an important tweak to the algorithm, which improves its accuracy and performance. Gradient Boosted Trees (GBT) is a generalized boosting algorithm introduced by Jerome Friedman. In contrast to the AdaBoost.M1 algorithm, GBT can deal with both multiclass classification and regression problems. Moreover, it can use any differential loss function, some popular ones are implemented. Decision trees usage as base learners allows processing ordered and categorical variables. Gradient Boosted Trees model represents an ensemble of single regression trees built in a greedy fashion. Training procedure is an iterative process similar to the numerical optimization via the gradient descent method. Summary loss on the training set depends only on the current model predictions for the training samples. At every training step, a single regression tree is built to predict antigradient vector components. Step length is computed corresponding to the loss function and separately for every region determined by the tree leaf. It can be eliminated by changing values of the leaves directly. The training process is given below in fig 5.5.

Step 1: Find the best constant model

Step 2: For i in [1,M]

    ○   Compute the antigradient

    ○   Grow a regression tree for predicting antigradient

    ○   Change the values in the tree leaves

    ○   Add the tree to the model

Step 3: The Result

$$f(x) = f_0 + v.\sum_{i=1}^{M} T_i(x)$$

Figure 5.5: Gradient Boosting

5.4.4. Genetic Algorithm

A Genetic Algorithm is a probabilistic search technique that computationally simulates the process of biological evolution. It mimics evolution in nature by repeatedly altering a population of candidate solutions until an optimal solution is found. The GA evolutionary cycle starts with a randomly selected initial population. The changes to the population occur through the processes of selection based on fitness, and alteration using crossover and mutation. The application of selection and alteration leads to a population with a higher proportion of better solutions. The evolutionary cycle continues until an acceptable solution is found in the current generation of population, or some control parameter such as the number of generations is exceeded. The smallest unit of a genetic algorithm is called a *gene*, which represents a unit of information in the problem domain. A series of genes, known as a *chromosome*, represents one possible solution to the problem. Each gene in the chromosome represents one component of the solution pattern. The most common form of representing a solution as a chromosome is a string of binary digits. Each bit in this string is a gene. The process of converting the solution from its original form into the bit string is known as *coding*. The specific coding scheme used is application dependent. The solution bit strings are decoded to enable their evaluation using a fitness measure.

Selection in biological evolution, only the fittest survive and their gene pool contributes to the creation of the next generation. Selection in GA is also based on a similar process. In a common form of selection, known as *fitness proportional selection*, each chromosome's likelihood of being selected as a good one is proportional to its fitness value. The alteration step in the genetic algorithm refines the good solution from the current generation to produce the next generation of candidate solutions. It is carried out by performing crossover and mutation.

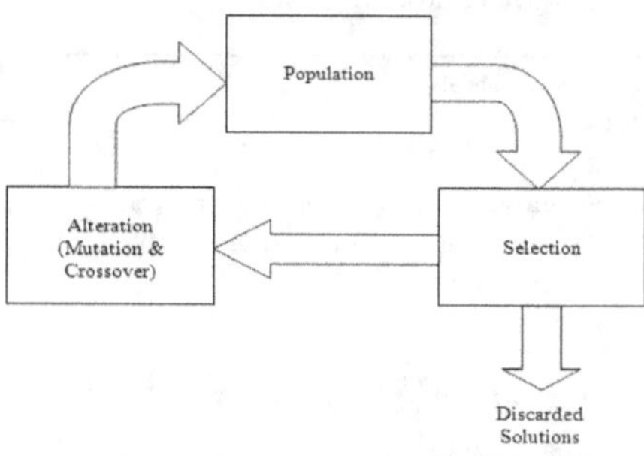

Figure 5.6: Genetic Algorithm

Crossover may be regarded as artificial mating in which chromosomes from two individuals are combined to create the chromosome for the next generation. This is done by splicing two chromosomes from two different solutions at a crossover point and swapping the spliced parts. The idea is that some genes with good characteristics from one chromosome may as a result combine with some good genes in the other chromosome to create a better solution represented by the new chromosome. **Mutation** is a random adjustment in the genetic composition. It is useful for introducing new characteristics in a population – something not achieved through crossover alone. Crossover only rearranges existing characteristics to give new combinations. For example, if the first bit in every chromosome of a generation happens to be a 1, any new chromosome created through crossover will also have 1 as the first bit. The mutation operator changes the current value of a gene to a different one. For bit string chromosome this change amounts to flipping a 0 bit to a 1 or vice versa. Although useful for introducing new traits in the solution pool, mutations can be counterproductive, and applied only infrequently and randomly. The steps in the typical Genetic Algorithm for finding a solution to a problem are listed below in fig 5.8.

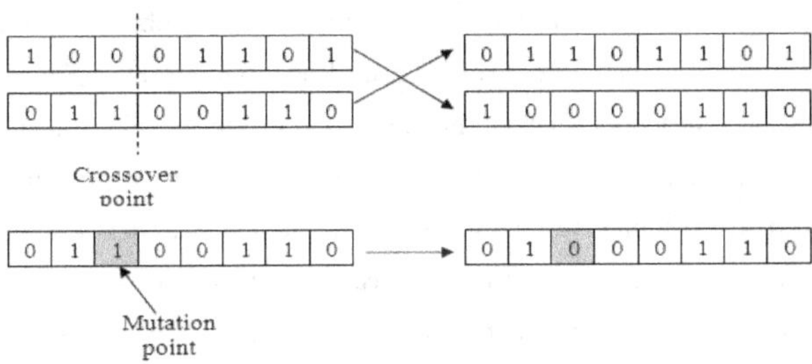

Figure 5.7: Crossover and Mutation Operation Performed in GA

1. Create an initial solution population of a certain size randomly
2. Evaluate each solution in the current generation and assign it a fitness value.
3. Select "good" solutions based on fitness value and discard the rest.
4. If acceptable solution(s) found in the current generation or maximum number of generations is exceeded then stop.
5. Alter the solution population using crossover and mutation to create a new generation of solutions.
6. Go to step 2.

Figure 5.8: Genetic Algorithm

5.4.5. k- Nearest Neighbor Algorithm

k-Nearest Neighbor Algorithm (k-NN) is a method for classifying data based on closest training examples in the feature space. k-NN is a type of instance-based learning, or lazy learning where the function is only approximated locally and all computation is deferred until classification. It can also be used for regression. The **k-NN** is amongst the simplest of all machine learning algorithms. An object is classified by a majority vote of its neighbors, with the object being assigned the class most common amongst its k nearest neighbors. k is a positive integer, typically small. If $k = 1$, then the object is simply assigned the class of its nearest neighbor. In binary (two class) classification problems, it is helpful to choose k to be an odd number as this avoids difficulties with tied votes.

The same method can be used for regression, by simply assigning the property value for the object to be the average of the values of its k-Nearest Neighbors. It can be useful to weight the contributions of the neighbors, so that the nearer neighbors contribute more to the average than the more distant ones. The neighbors are taken from a set of objects for which the correct classification is known. This can be thought of as the training set for the algorithm, though no explicit training step is required. In order to identify neighbors, the objects are represented by position vectors in a multidimensional feature space. It is usual to use the Euclidean distance, though other distance measures, such as the Manhattan distance could in principle be used instead. The k-Nearest Neighbor algorithm is sensitive to the local structure of the data. The test sample (green circle) should be classified either to the first class of blue squares or to the second class of red triangles. If $k = 3$ it is classified to the second class because there are 2 triangles and only 1 square inside the inner circle. If $k = 5$ it is classified to first class (3 squares vs. 2 triangles inside the outer circle).The training examples are vectors in a multidimensional feature space. The space is partitioned into regions by locations and labels of the training samples. A point in the space is assigned to the class c if it is the most frequent class label among the k nearest training samples. Usually Euclidean distance is used. The training phase of the algorithm consists only of storing the feature vectors and class labels of the training samples.

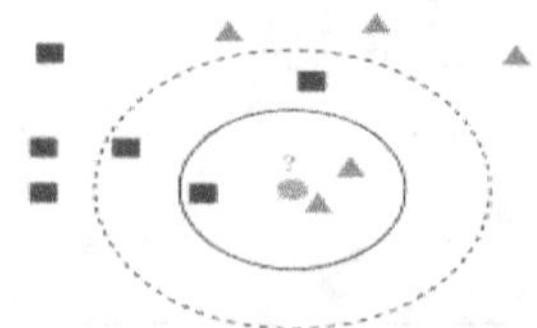

Figure 5.9: Example of k-NN Classification

In the actual classification phase, the test sample (whose class is not known) is represented as a vector in the feature space. Distances from the new vector to all stored vectors are computed and k closest samples are selected. There are a number of ways to classify the new vector to a particular class, one of the most used technique is to predict the new vector to the most common class amongst the k-nearest neighbors. A major drawback to use this technique to classify a new vector to a class is that the classes with the more frequent examples tend to dominate the prediction of the new vector, as they tend to come up in the k-nearest neighbors when the neighbors are computed due to their large number. One of the ways to overcome this problem is to take into account the distance of each k-nearest neighbor with the new vector that is to be classified and predict the class of the new vector based on these distances.

Parameter selection is the best choice of k depends upon the data; generally, larger values of k reduce the effect of noise on the classification, but make boundaries between classes less distinct. A good k can be selected by various heuristic techniques, for example, cross-validation. The special case where the class is predicted to be the class of the closest training sample (i.e. when $k = 1$) is called the nearest neighbor algorithm. The accuracy of the k-NN algorithm can be severely degraded by the presence of noisy or irrelevant features, or if the feature scales are not consistent with their importance. Much research effort has been put into selecting or scaling features to improve classification. A particularly popular approach is the use of evolutionary algorithms to optimize feature scaling. Another popular approach is to scale features by the mutual information of the training data with the training classes.

Properties The naive version of the algorithm is easy to implement by computing the distances from the test sample to all stored vectors, but it is computationally intensive, especially when the size of the training set grows. Many optimizations have been proposed over the years; these generally seek to reduce the number of distance evaluations actually performed. Some optimizations involve partitioning the feature space, and only computing distances within specific nearby volumes. Several different types of nearest neighbor finding algorithms include: Linear scan, Kd-trees, Balltrees, Metric trees, Locality sensitive hashing (LSH), Agglomerative-Nearest-Neighbor. The Nearest Neighbor Algorithm has some strong consistency results. As the amount of data approaches infinity, the algorithm is guaranteed to yield an error rate no worse than twice the Bayes error rate (the minimum achievable error rate given the distribution of the data). k-Nearest Neighbor is guaranteed to approach the Bayes error rate, for some value of k (where k increases as a function of the number of data points). The k-NN algorithm can also be adapted for use in estimating continuous variables.

One such implementation uses an inverse distance weighted average of the k-Nearest Multivariate Neighbors. This algorithm functions as follows in fig 5.10.

1   Compute Euclidean or Mahalanobis distance from target plot to those that were sampled.

2   Order samples taking for account calculated distances.

3   Choose heuristically optimal k nearest neighbor based on RMSE done by cross validation technique.

4   Calculate an inverse distance weighted average with the k-nearest multivariate neighbors

Figure 5.10: k-Nearest Neighbor Algorithm

5.4.6. *Ripper Algorithm*

The Repeated Incremental Pruning to Produce Error Reduction (Ripper) is a classification algorithm designed to generate rules set directly from the training dataset. The name is drawn from the fact that the rules are learned incrementally. A new rule associated with a class value will cover various attributes of that class. The algorithm was designed to be fast and effective when dealing with large and noisy datasets compared to decision trees. During the growing phase of the algorithm, a greedy approach of learning is applied, i.e. each rule is learned one at a time. In datasets with very large dimensions, this causes over-fitting of the data. This in turn increases the classification error rate significantly if the algorithm is tested with data with missing values.

The Ripper model is not as popular as the decision trees in the insurance domain, but it has been applied in financial risk analysis. It has been used in financial institutes to help find the best policy for credit products, increase revenue as well as decreasing losses. Ripper Algorithm involves the below stages and explained clearly in fig 5.11. Building Stage repeats 2 and 3 until the Description Length (DL) of the rule set and examples is 64 bits greater than the smallest DL met so far, or there are no positive examples, or the error rate is greater equal than 50 percent. Grow Phase grows one rule by greedily adding antecedents (or conditions) to the rule until the rule is perfect (i.e. 100 percent accurate). The procedure checks every possible value of each attribute and selects the condition with high information gain. Prune Phase incrementally prune each rule and allow the pruning of any final sequences of the antecedents.

Optimization Stage after generating the initial rule set, generate and prune two variants of each rule from randomized data using procedure 2 and 3. But one variant is generated from an empty rule while the other one is generated by greedily adding antecedents to the original rule. Moreover, the pruning metric used is. Then the smallest possible DL for each variant and the original rule is computed. The variant with the minimal DL is selected as the final representative of in the ruleset. After all the rules in have been examined and if there are still residual positives, more rules are generated based on the residual positives using Building Stage again. Delete the rules from the ruleset that would increase the DL of the entire ruleset if it were in it, and add resultant ruleset. (Zantema and Bodlaender, 2000)

```
Input: Training dataset S with n instances and m attributes

Output: Ruleset

begin
  sort classes in the order of least prevalent class
  to the most prevalent class.
  create a new rule set
    while iterating from the prevalent class to the
        most prevalent class
        split S into into Spos and Sneg
    while Spos is not empty
  split Spos and Sneg into Gpos and Gneg subsets
  and Ppos and Pneg subsets.
  create and prune a new rule
    if the error rate of the new rule is very
  large then
      end while
      else
  add new rule to rule set
  the total description length l is
  computed
    if l > d then
        end while
      end while
    end while
  end
```

Figure 5.11: Ripper Algorithm

5.4.7. *Modified Ripper Algorithm*

RIPPER was introduced as a successor of the Incremental Reduced Error Pruning (IREP) algorithm for rule induction. Even though the key principles remain the same, MRIPPER improves IREP in many details and is also able to cope with multiclass problems. A single MRIPPER rule consists of an antecedent part and a consequent part. The antecedent part is a conjunction of predicates (selectors) and the consequent part is a class assignment. MRIPPER learns such rules in a greedy manner, following a separate-and-conquer strategy. Prior to the learning process, the training data are sorted by class labels in ascending order according to the corresponding class frequencies. Rules are then learned for the first $m - 1$ classes, starting with the smallest one. Once a rule has been created, the instances covered by that rule is removed from the training data, and this is repeated until no instances from the target classes are left. The algorithm then proceeds with the next class. Finally MRIPPER finds no more rules to learn, a default rule (with empty antecedent) is added for the last (and hence, most frequent) class. Rules for single classes are learned until either all positive instances are covered or the last rule has been added was "too complicated." The latter property is implemented in terms of the total description length: the stopping condition is fulfilled if the description length of r is at least d bits longer than the shortest description length encountered so far are shown in figure 5.12.

```
procedure BUILDSET(P,N)
P = positive examples
N = negative examples
RuleSet = {}
DL = Deseriptiontength(RuleSet, P, N)
while P ≠ {}
        // Grow and prune a new rule
        split (P, N) into (Grow Pas, Grow Neg) and (PrunePos, Prune Neg)
        Rule := GrowRule(Grow Pos, Grow Neg)
        Rule := PruneRule(Rule, Prune Pos, Prune Neg)
        add Rule to RuleSet
        if DescriptionLength(RuteSet, P, N) > DL + 69 then
                // Prune the whole rule set and exit
                for each rule R in RuleSet (considered in reverse order)
                        if DescriptionLength(RuleSet {R}, P, N) < DL then
                                delete R from RuleSet
                                DL := DescriptionLength(RuleSet, P, N)
                        end if
                end for
                return (RuleSet)
                end if
        DL := DescriptionLength(RuleSet, P, N)
        delete from P and N all examples covered by Rule
        end while
end BUILDRULESET
procedure OPTIM IZERULESET(RuleSet, P, N)
for each rule R in RuleSet
        delete R from RuleSet
        U Pos := examples in P not covered by RuleSet
        U Neg := examples in N not covered by RuleSet
        split (U Pos,U Neg) into (Grow Pos, Grow Neg) and (Prune Pos, PruneNeg)
        Rep Rule := GrowRule(GrowPos,GrowNeg)
        Rep Rule := PruneRule(Rep Rule, Prune Pos, Prune Neg)
        Rev Rule := GrowRule(GrowPos,GrowNeg,R)
        Rev Rule := PruneRule(Rev Rule, PrunePos,PruneNeg)
        choose better of Rep Rule and Rev Rule and add to RuleSet
end for
end OPTIMIZERCIESET

procedure RIP PER( P, N, k)
RuleSet := BUILDRULESET(P, N)
repeat k times RuleSet := OPTIMIZERULESET(RuleS et, P, N)
return (RuleSet)
end RIPPER
```

Figure 5.12: Modified Ripper Algorithm

Sampling Methods Used

Oversampling and undersampling in data analysis are techniques used to adjust the class distribution of a data set (i.e. the ratio between the different classes/categories represented). Oversampling and undersampling are opposite and roughly equivalent techniques. They both involve using a bias to select more samples from one class than from another. The usual reason for oversampling is to correct for a bias in the original dataset. One scenario where it is useful is when training a classifier using labeled training data from a biased source, since labeled training data is valuable but often comes from un-representative sources.

A number of resampling methods have been proposed and studied in the past. Resampling methods can be divided into two categories: oversampling methods and undersampling methods. Oversampling methods balance training class priors by increasing the number of minority class data points, while undersampling methods balance training class priors by decreasing the number of majority class data points. Some widely used approaches are random oversampling, random undersampling, and cost-proportionate rejection sampling. Random oversampling increases the number of minority class data points in the training set by randomly replicating existing minority class members. While simplistic, random oversampling has performed well in empirical studies even when compared to other, more complicated oversampling methods. Unfortunately, since random oversampling only replicates existing data points, it has been argued that random oversampling does not add any actual data to the training set. Instead of replicating existing data points, "synthetic" minority class members are added to the training set by creating new data points. Empirically, SMOTE has shown to perform well against random oversampling.

In SMOTE, a new data point is created from an existing data point as follows: find the n nearest neighbors to the existing data point; randomly select one of the n nearest neighbors; the new, synthetic point is a randomly chosen point on the line segment joining the original data point and its randomly chosen neighbor. In this paper, we introduce an oversampling method which also adds information to the training set by creating synthetic minority class points. Our method requires the choice of a probability distribution to model the minority class. Random undersampling decreases the number of majority class data points by randomly eliminating majority class data points currently in the training set. Like random oversampling, random undersampling has empirically performed well despite its simplicity. A disadvantage of undersampling is that it removes potentially useful information from the training set. For example, since it indiscriminately removes points, it does not consider the difference between points close to the potential decision boundary and points very far from the decision boundary.

A more sophisticated undersampling method with nice theoretical property is cost-proportionate rejection sampling. Cost-proportionate rejection sampling is based on a theorem that describes how to turn any classifier which reduces the number of misclassification errors into a cost-sensitive classifier. Given that each data point has a misclassification cost c, each data point in the training set has probability c=z of being included in the resampled training set, where z is a user-defined parameter (e.g., let z equal the largest value of c in the training set in order to maximize the expected size of the resampled dataset). Advanced Random Under Sampling can be used in any domain where there exist probability distributions that model the actual data distributions well. Advanced Random Under Sampling works as follows: A probability distribution is chosen to model the minority class, Based on the training data, parameters for the probability distribution are learned and artificial data points are added to the resampled data set by generating points from the learned probability distribution until the desired number of minority class points in the training set has been reached. The idea behind Advanced Random Under Sampling is simple, straightforward, and is a natural approach in data mining and machine learning. Indeed, the idea of creating artificial data points through a probability distribution with learned parameters has been used for many other applications.

5.5. Summary

Customer churn is one among the major research topics in customer relationship management. Several approaches were proposed for customer churn prediction. This chapter discussed the various techniques for predicting customer churn, comparison with other techniques that deals with the concerned research problem. The next chapter deals with the development of prototype.

CHAPTER 6

DEVELOPMENT AND TESTING OF MODIFIED RIPPER ALGORITHM AND CASE STUDY

6.1. Introduction

Retail banks often deal with customer churn. Among the several issues addressed by Customer Relationship Management (CRM), identifying the customers who are about to quit the relationship with a company is one of the most important in the financial services industry. When competition becomes tougher, when laws decrease either the barriers to entry or the customer's switching costs, or when a company aims at strengthening its position in a new market, the issue of retaining customers and avoiding customer churn becomes even more crucial. In the last decade several computer science scholars have tackled the problem of building accurate models to identify customers at risk in a bank by using statistical, machine learning and data mining approaches. However, much literature only focuses on the problem of correctly predicting that a customer is about to switch.

Very rarely the problem of generating personalized actions to improve customer retention rates is considered. The decision of what actions to deliver to what customers is normally left to managers who can only rely upon their knowledge. However, these decisions are at least as critical as the correct identification of customer at risk. A customer churn prediction model should be integrated with a model to decide what personalized marketing action to deliver to customers; otherwise the benefits of using accurate predictive models would be lost. This chapter discusses on the design and development of algorithms used in this research. This chapter introduces about the banking dataset towards customer churn prediction. The screenshots that have been of the outcome of this research is compared and discussions will be made. The tables are described briefly following with the summary.

6.2. Case Study-Banking

Acquiring new customers is a more costly process than retaining existing customers. Therefore, the management of relationship with customers plays a vital role in improving the overall profitability of a company. There are many segments that come under the Customer Relationship Management (CRM) umbrella such as churn prediction, target marketing, cross/up selling, customer profiling, etc. *Churn* is defined as the propensity of a customer to cease doing business with a company in a given time period. This paper emphasize on modeling churn behavior of bank customer. High cost of customer acquisition and customer education requires companies to make large upfront investments on customers. However, due to easy access to information and a wide range of offerings, it is easier than ever before for customers to switch between service providers. This applies to all industry verticals such as banking, telecom, insurance, etc. Therefore, customer churn, which is defined as the propensity of customers to cease doing business with a company in a given time period, has become a significant problem and is one of the prime challenges financial institutions worldwide are learning to face. Studies reveal that customer churn is a costly affair. Identifying the churn before hand and taking necessary steps to retain them (customer retention) would increase the overall profitability of the company.

A study conducted in reveal that a bank is able to increase its profits by 85% due to a 5% improvement in the retention rate. Similar findings emerged in, who calculated the financial impact of an increase in retention rate of 1%. Another study conducted in says that losing customers not only leads to opportunity costs because of reduced sales, but also to an increased need for attracting new customers, which is five to six times more expensive than customer retention. In the banking industry, identifying probable churn customers has increased in its importance in the recent past. In banking domain, we define a churn customer as one who closes all his/her accounts and stops doing business with the bank. There are many reasons for a customer to close the account(s). For example, a person creates an account for a specific purpose and closes it immediately after the purpose is solved. Or a person is relocated and has to move to another place and hence closes all the accounts. Or a customer may stop transacting with the bank just because of the unavailability of bank's ATMs in important places and hence close his/her accounts. The problem here is that, in real world scenario, the bank does not always capture this kind of feedback data. Hence, no further analysis can be done and this type of churning behaviours could not be stopped. This leaves us in a situation where we need to think which kind of churn patterns are possible to identify. Hence prediction of churn becomes a very challenging problem in banking sector. Very often, we need to live with the raw customer data available and extract the churn patterns out of it. So it can be said that the problem of predicting churn is divided into two steps viz., convert the raw data into meaningful data and convert the meaningful data into knowledge.

Raw data available in real-time banking scenario, provide a guideline to convert raw data into meaningful data and finally convert the meaningful data into knowledge using predictive data mining techniques. This is a dataset from a Bank with approximately 100.000 of non credit card holders in a tab delimited text file. Product balances & transactions are the main attributes of this dataset. The dependent variable is the spontaneous activation of a new credit card. All customer attributes have been collected before the activation of the new credit card. It can be used for deriving new variables, descriptive analysis, association analysis and ropensity modelling for finding new target groups for new credit cards promotion. The following are the attributes of the dataset and sample dataset is depicted in Fig. 6.1.

- Customer_id
- Gender
- Age
- Tenure
- Saving_amount
- Current_amount
- Time_deposits_amount
- Funds_amount
- Stocks_amount
- Bank_assurance_amount
- Life_assurance_amount

Customer_ID	Gender	Age	Tenure	Saving_Amount	Current_Amount	Time_Deposits_Amount	Funds_Amount	Stocks_Amount	Bank_Assurance_Amount	Life_Assurance_Amount
25415	M	34	69	1733.35	134.66	0.00	0.00	482.29	403.74	0.00
25416	F	49	69	0.00	0.00	0.00	0.00	0.00	0.00	103.82
25417	M	29	69	11.65	0.00	0.00	0.00	0.00	0.00	0.00
25418	M	45	69	1149.86	0.00	288513.57	0.00	0.00	0.00	0.00
25419	F	36	69	30.19	2543.48	0.00	0.00	15.47	0.00	0.00
25420	M	56	69	8838.77	0.00	0.00	0.00	0.00	0.00	0.00
25421	M	31	69	20435.48	0.00	2919.35	0.00	0.00	0.00	0.00
25422	F	51	69	0.00	21.46	0.00	0.00	0.00	0.00	28.18
25423	M	58	69	14192.97	0.00	0.00	10238.19	58165.63	0.00	0.00
25424	M	66	69	1464.14	0.00	0.00	0.00	0.00	0.00	0.00
25425	M	58	69	0.00	0.00	0.00	0.00	0.00	0.00	0.00
25426	F	40	69	21.62	0.00	0.00	0.00	0.00	0.00	0.00
25427	M	61	69	0.00	2145.93	0.00	0.00	0.00	0.00	0.00
25428	F	68	69	0.00	0.00	0.00	0.00	951.82	0.00	0.00
25429	F	40	69	0.00	185.94	0.00	0.00	0.00	0.00	0.00
25430	M	67	69	629.41	0.00	0.00	0.00	0.00	0.00	0.00
25431	F	40	69	0.00	0.00	0.00	0.00	0.00	0.00	0.00
25432	F	65	69	227.11	0.00	0.00	0.00	5070.81	0.00	0.00
25433	M	65	69	0.00	0.00	0.00	0.00	15029.16	0.00	0.00
25434	M	27	69	571.66	0.00	0.00	0.00	0.00	0.00	0.00
25435	F	49	69	0.00	0.00	0.00	0.00	0.00	0.00	0.00
25436	M	71	69	123.50	0.00	14597.39	11756.25	0.00	0.00	0.00
25437	F	32	69	0.00	71.43	0.00	0.00	0.00	0.00	0.00
25438	M	58	69	480.14	0.00	0.00	0.00	0.00	0.00	0.00
25439	F	61	69	0.00	0.00	0.00	0.00	446.86	0.00	0.00
25440	F	54	69	1959.22	246.72	0.00	0.00	0.00	0.00	0.00
25441	M	49	69	0.00	0.00	0.00	0.00	0.00	0.00	0.00
25442	M	67	69	0.00	0.00	0.00	0.00	0.00	0.00	0.00
25443	M	45	69	22.77	0.00	0.00	0.00	1815.05	0.00	0.00
25444	M	60	69	20.19	0.00	0.00	0.00	0.00	299.29	315.04

Figure 6.1: Sample Dataset

To Find Customer Behaviour Approache Followed in Banks

Five main categories can be identified to classify the approaches to the generation of personalized actions. Each category represents a set of homogeneous approaches which can be used to decide what action should be delivered to what customers in a bank. The following approaches clearly illustrate the customer's ideas and their thinking in various aspects. Computational approach includes all those approaches that build a complete model of customers' behaviour, actions, and customers' reactions based on information stored in a data set. These approaches can use both data mining (Wang and Jiang, 2006) and optimization models (Zhang and Wedel, 2009; Ansari and Mela, 2003; Pancras and Sudhir, 2007). An example of applications in banking and finance is a retail bank which stores the data related to promotion of stocks, and the reactions of customers who might have purchased those stocks or not. The fundamental condition that enables the adoption of these approaches is the completeness of data. If the data sets do not include, for instance, the reaction of each customer to a certain marketing campaign, then neither a mining algorithm nor an optimization model can be run to generate personalized actions. Computational approaches allow a company to fully automate the generation of actions based on customers' profiles, as no human decision is needed. A limitation is that only marketing actions already launched before can be considered in such approach. The full coverage of customers may be another problem because some customers' reactions may remain unknown for instance, when a customer does not respond to a survey.

Similarity-Based approach is used by Recommender Systems (Linden et al., 2003) and Web content personalization methods (Mobasher et al., 2001). This kind of approach assumes that actions are related to customer preferences, preferences may be inferred by customer profiles, and that either similar customers behave similarly or similar actions cause similar reactions. A "similarity-based" approach does not require to store as much information as a computational approach. Recording customers' preferences is enough, because it is assumed that the unknown preferences of a customer can be derived by identifying the similarity with other customers. However, the twofold condition of applicability of such approaches is that customers' profiles have to represent preferences, and only actions associated with those preferences can be generated. For instance, a customer who owns multiple credit cards can be classified as a customer who "prefers" using credit cards, whereas the fact that a customer has a mort-gage does not necessarily represent a "preference". A "similarity-based" approach is useful to automate the personalization process. Bottom-Up approach includes the knowledge discovery methods (Mobasher et al., 2001, Tuzhilin and Adomavicius, 2001) and the use of front office personnel. These approaches consist of two separate steps: 1) pro-filing customers, 2) deciding proper actions, where the first step has to precede the second step (i.e., actions depend on profiles). They cannot be fully made automatic because only the first step is performed by an algorithm. For this reason these approaches are typically not very efficient. The condition of applicability is that the decision-making effort has not to exceed the company's re-sources: either the number of customers is low or the number of decision-makers are high. The advantage is that targeting can be very effective because each profile is thoroughly analyzed before generating a proper action. An example of bottom-up approach in banking is the work of a financial advisor who manages a portfolio of customers. The advisor has periodic conversations with a customer, analyzes her needs and proposes tailored financial solutions.

Top-Down approache includes the direct marketing approaches (Reinartz and Venkatesan, 2009). They consist of the same two separate steps typical in bottom-up approaches. However, in this case, the decision of what actions to deliver is made before the definition of customers' profiles and, hence, pro-files depend on actions. For instance, a retail bank managers may first decide to offer customers a discount on bank transfers, and then select the target customers by building appropriate profiles.

Table 6.1: Approaches to the Definition of Personalized Retention Actions

Approach & Characteristics	Conditions	Benefits	Risks
Computational Complete model of preferences, actions and reactions.	The data set includes information on prior marketing actions and customers' responses	• Control • Automation • Targeting	• Limited scope of actions • Customer coverage
Similarity-Based Comparison between customer profiles	Actions are related to customer preferences, and preferences may be inferred by customer profiles	• Control • Automation • Efficiency • Coverage	• Limited scope of actions
Bottom-Up The definition of customers' profiles precedes the definition of actions	The supervision effort has to be affordable (in terms of number of profiles and resources)	• Targeting •Scope of actions • Coverage	• Low efficiency • Lack of control
Top-Down The definition of customers' profiles follows the definition of actions	Actions can be defined independently of customers' profiles	• Control • Efficiency	• Lack of targeting • Limited coverage of customers
Customization Customers are free to choose the appropriate action.	The offer has to be granular enough	• Targeting	• Low efficiency • Lack of control

The condition of applicability is that actions can be de-fined before customers' profiles. In some CRM problems, such as reducing customer churn, this condition can be questionable. **Customization Approach** offer customers many different options and let the customers choose the suitable one. This approach is typically adopted in mass customization (Kumar, 2007). In this approach actions do not derive from processing customers' profiles but rather from customers' choices. This makes customization different from other personalization approaches (Arora et al., 2008).The offer has to be granular enough in order to adopt this approach. For instance, a retail bank can propose customers to choose one among many discounted options (e.g., a discount on bank transfers, credit cards, cash cards, e-transactions, etc.). The association between actions and profiles is performed by the customers instead of the company. For this reason, the control over the process is low and the resulting actions can turn out to be quite expensive. However, the targeting is expected to be quite effective.

6.3.   Handling Class Imbalance

Weiss (2004) draws up six categories of problems that arise when mining imbalanced classes.

1. **Improper evaluation metrics**: often, not the best metrics are used to guide the data mining algorithms and to evaluate the results of data mining.

2. **Lack of data: absolute rarity:** the number of examples associated with the rare class is small in an absolute sense, which makes it difficult to detect regularities within the rare class.

3. **Relative lack of data**: relative rarity: objects are not rare in absolute sense, but are rare relative to other objects, which makes it hard for greedy search heuristics, and more global methods are, in general, not tractable.

4. **Data fragmentation:** Many data mining algorithms, like decision trees, employ a divide-and-conquer approach, where the original problem is decomposed into smaller and smaller problems, which results in the instance space being partitioned into smaller and smaller pieces. This is a problem because regularities can then only be found within each individual partition, which will contain less data.

5. **Inappropriate inductive bias:** Generalizing from specific examples, or induction, requires an extra-evidentiary bias. Without such a bias "inductive leaps" are not possible and learning cannot occur. The bias of a data mining system is therefore critical to its performance. Many learners utilize a general bias in order to foster generalization and avoid over fitting. This bias can adversely impact the ability to learn rare cases and rare classes.

6. **Noise:** Noisy data will affect the way any data mining system behaves, but interesting is that noise has a greater impact on rare cases than on common cases.

6.4. Evaluation Metrics

Classification Accuracy is often hard or nearly impossible to construct a perfect classification model that would correctly classify all examples from the test set. Therefore, we have to choose a suboptimal classification model that best suits our needs and works best on our problem domain. In our case, we could use a classifier that makes a binary prediction (i.e. the customer will either stay with the company or not) or a classifier that gives a probabilistic class prediction to which class an example belongs. The first is called binary classifier and the latter is called probabilistic classifier. One can easily turn a probabilistic classifier into a binary one using a certain threshold traditionally so that the Yrate in the test set is equal to the churn rate in the original training set. Binary Classifiers always label one class as a positive (in our case a churner) and the other one as a negative class (a non churner). The test set consists of P positive and N negative examples. A classifier assigns a class to each of them, but some of the assignments are wrong. To assess the classification results we count the number of true positive (TP), true negative (TN), false positive (FP) (actually negative, but classified as positive) and false negative (FN) (actually positive, but classified as negative) examples. It holds

$$TP+FN=P \text{ and } TN+FP=N$$

The classifier assigned TP + FP examples to the positive class and TN + FN examples to the negative class. Let us define a few well known and widely used measures:

$$specificity = \frac{TN}{N} \Rightarrow 1 - \frac{FP}{N} = FPrate$$

$$sensitivity = \frac{TN}{P} = FPrate = recall$$

$$Yrate = \frac{TP + FP}{P + N}$$

$$precision = \frac{TP}{TP + FP}$$

$$Accuracy = \frac{TP + TN}{P + N}$$

$$\Rightarrow misclassifcation \ error \ (MER) = 1 - accuracy$$

Precision, recall and accuracy (or MER) are often used to measure the classification quality of binary classifiers. The FPrate measures the fraction of non churners that are misclassified as churners. The TPrate or recall measures the fraction of churners correctly classified. Precision measures that fraction of examples classified as churner that are truly churner. Area under ROC curve is often used as a measure of quality of a probabilistic classifier. It is close to the perception of classification quality that most people have. AUC is computed with the following formula:

$$AUC = \int_0^1 \frac{TP}{P} \, d\frac{FP}{N} = \frac{1}{P.N} \int_0^N TPdFP$$

For each negative example count the number of positive examples with a higher assigned score than the negative example, sum it up and divide everything with P * N. This is exactly the same procedure as used to compute the probability that a random positive example has a higher assigned score than random negative example.

$$AUC = P(Score_{Random\ churner} > Score_{Random\ non\ churner})$$

In many data mining tasks, including churn prediction, it is the rare cases that are of primary interest. Metrics that do not take this into account generally do not perform well in these situations. One solution is to use cost-sensitive learning methods (Weiss, 2004). These methods can exploit the fact that the value of correctly identifying the positive (rare) class outweighs the value of correctly identifying the common class. For two-class problems this is done by associating a greater cost with false negatives than with false positives. Assigning a greater cost to false negatives than to false positives will improve performance with respect to the positive (rare) class. If this misclassification cost ratio is 3:1, then a region that has ten negative examples and four positive examples will nonetheless be labeled with the positive class. Thus non-uniform costs can bias the classifier to perform well on the positive class where in this case the bias is desirable.

Weighted Random Forests classifier tends to be biased towards the majority class, one can place a heavier penalty on misclassifying the minority class (Chen et al., 2004). A weight is assigned to each class, with the minority class given larger weight (i.e., higher misclassification cost). The class weights are incorporated into the RF algorithm in two places. In the tree induction procedure, class weights are used to weight the Gini criterion for finding splits. In the terminal nodes of each tree, class weights are again taken into consideration. The class prediction of each terminal node is determined by "weighted majority vote"; i.e., the weighted vote of a class is the weight for that class times the number of cases for that class at the terminal node. The final class prediction for RF is then determined by aggregating the weighted vote from each individual tree, where the weights are average weights in the terminal nodes. Class weights are an essential tuning parameter to achieve desired performance. The out-of-bag estimate of the accuracy from RF can be used to select weights.

A Decision Tree is a tree act upon in which each branch node represents a choice between a number of different nodes and each leaf node represents a decision. Decision Trees are used for gaining information for the intention of decision making. Based on decision tree learning algorithm, the tree starts with a root node on which it is for users to take actions. From the node, users split each node recursively. The ultimate result is a decision tree in which each branch represents a possible scenario of decision and its outcome. Decision Tree learning is a method for approximating discrete valued target functions, in which the learned function is represented by a decision tree. Decision Tree learning is the one of the most widely used and practical methods for inductive inference. It has been successfully used in expert systems in capturing knowledge.

The main task performed in these systems is using inductive methods to the given values of attributes of an unknown object to determine appropriate classification based on decision tree rules. Decision Trees classify requests by traverse from root node to leaf node. The user start from root node of decision tree, testing the attribute specified by the node and then moving down the tree branch based on the attribute value in the given set. This process is repeated at the sub-tree level. The Decision Tree learning algorithm to be suited for request is represented as attribute value pairs. For example, attribute 'Temperature' and its value 'hot', 'mild', 'cool'. The user are concerning to extend attribute -value to continuous-valued data numeric attribute value. The target function has discrete output values. It can easily deal with instance which is assigned to a Boolean decision, such as true or false, 'p (positive)' and 'n (negative)'. The training data may contain errors. This can be dealt with pruning techniques. Boosting is a technique for improving the accuracy of a predictive function by applying the function repeatedly in a series and combining the output of each function with weighting so that the total error of the prediction is minimized. In many cases, the predictive accuracy of such a series greatly exceeds the accuracy of the base function used alone. The first popular boosting algorithm was AdaBoost, short for adaptive boosting, by Freund and Schapire, 1997. It is a meta-algorithm, and can be used in con- junction with many other learning algorithms to improve their performance.

AdaBoost is adaptive in the sense that subsequent classifiers built are tweaked in favour of those instances misclassified by previous classifiers. Gradient boosting constructs additive regression models by sequentially fitting a simple parameterized function (base learner) to current "pseudo"-residuals by least squares at each iteration. The pseudo-residuals are the gradient of the loss function being minimized, with respect to the model values at each training data point evaluated at the current step. It is shown that both the approximation accuracy and execution speed of gradient boosting can be substantially improved by incorporating randomization into the procedure. Specifically, at each iteration a sub sample of the training data is drawn at random (without replacement) from the full training data set.

Table 6.2: Random Over Sampling for DT, GB and WRF Algorithms

Algorithm	Metrics	10	20	30	40	50	60	70	80	90	100
DT	AUC	0.0080	0.0363	0.0960	0.1473	0.2355	0.3040	0.4281	0.5633	0.7182	0.9086
	ERROR	0.2500	0.2632	0.3484	0.3625	0.3643	0.3800	0.4000	0.4080	0.4286	0.4308
	ACCU	56.9231	57.1429	59.2000	60.0000	62.0000	63.5714	63.7500	65.1613	73.6842	75.0000
GB	AUC	0.0114	0.0416	0.0929	0.1480	0.2365	0.3116	0.4298	0.5690	0.7171	0.9082
	ERR	0.1600	0.1760	0.1274	0.1353	0.1229	0.1399	0.1740	0.1587	0.1435	0.1324
	ACC	83.1579	84.5455	84.6154	85.6000	85.7143	85.7143	6.2500	87.0968	88.0000	90.0000
WRF	AUC	0.0142	0.0550	0.0878	0.6313	0.2960	0.4221	0.4645	0.4635	0.8300	0.8703
	ERR	0.2000	0.2960	0.3000	0.3077	0.3429	0.3800	0.4065	0.4250	0.4842	0.50710
	ACC	49.2857	51.5789	57.5000	59.3548	62.0000	65.7143	69.2308	70.0000	70.4000	80.0000

Table 6.2 shows the performance of various existing algorithms such as decision trees, gradient boosting and weighted random forest on random over sampling method. From the results of performance metric area under curve it is clear that decision tree performs better than the other algorithms such as decision tree and weighted random forest algorithms. It is clear that in almost all iterations from 10 to 100, the performance AUC is better in decision tree. This table also depicts the error performance of various existing algorithms such as decision trees, gradient boosting and weighted random forest on random over sampling method. From the results of performance metric error it is clear that gradient boosting reduces the error rate than the other algorithms such as decision tree and weighted random forest. Also, it is clear that in almost all iterations from 10 to 100, the performance error rate is reduced in gradient boosting method. The table shows the performance accuracy of the existing algorithms. From all the iterations it can be understood that the gradient boosting algorithm performs better than that of other algorithms. Graphical representation of the comparison is given in Fig. 6.2.

Table 6.3: Random Under Sampling for DT, GB and WRF Algorithms

Algorithm	Metrics	10	20	30	40	50	60	70	80	90	100
DT	AUC	0.0242	0.0722	0.1417	0.2558	0.3834	0.5654	0.7798	1.0018	1.2582	1.05654
	ERROR	0.1600	0.2000	0.2162	0.2207	0.2222	0.2381	0.2424	0.2488	0.2769	0.2824
	ACC	71.7647	72.3077	75.1220	75.7576	76.1905	77.7778	77.9310	78.3784	80.0000	84.0000
GB	AUC	0.0234	0.0750	0.1479	0.2572	0.3822	0.5711	0.7809	1.0072	1.2600	1.5633
	ERR	0.0800	0.1333	0.1366	0.1379	0.1394	0.1405	0.1440	0.1529	0.1538	0.1619
	ACC	72.8295	84.7354	84.5965	85.5300	85.3299	86.8606	86.7869	86.3285	86.3427	90.0000
WRF	AUC	0.3112	0.0760	0.0652	0.3121	0.7600	0.3320	0.5461	0.9124	0.8100	0.5210
	ERR	0.5600	0.5714	0.5727	0.6000	0.6357	0.6800	0.6947	0.7077	0.7625	0.8000
	ACC	20.0000	23.7500	29.2308	30.5263	32.0000	36.4286	40.0000	42.7273	42.8571	44.0000

Table 6.3 shows the performance of various existing algorithms such as decision trees, gradient boosting and weighted random forest on random over sampling method. From the results of performance metric area under curve it is clear that weighted random forest

performs better than the other algorithms such as decision tree and gradient boosting. It is clear that in almost all iterations from 10 to 100, the performance AUC is better in weighted random forest. This table also depicts the error performance of various existing algorithms such as decision trees, gradient boosting and weighted random forest on random over sampling method. From the results of performance metric error it is clear that gradient boosting reduces the error rate than the other algorithms such as decision tree and weighted random forest. Also, it is clear that in almost all iterations from 10 to 100, the performance error rate is reduced in gradient boosting method. The table shows the performance accuracy of the existing algorithms. From all the iterations it can be understood that the gradient boosting algorithm performs better than that of other algorithms. Graphical representation of the comparison is given in Fig. 6.2.

Table 6.4: Advanced Random Under Sampling for DT, GB and WRF Algorithms

Algorithm	Metrics	10	20	30	40	50	60	70	80	90	100
DT	AUC	0.0251	0.0676	0.1494	0.2517	0.3819	0.5683	0.7740	0.9999	1.2617	1.5632
	ERROR	0.1200	0.1440	0.1448	0.1512	0.1556	0.1568	0.1576	0.1692	0.1765	0.1810
	ACCU	81.9048	82.3529	83.0769	84.2424	84.3243	84.4444	84.8780	85.5172	85.6000	88.0000
GB	AUC	0.0247	0.0726	0.1476	0.2579	0.3831	0.5684	0.7797	1.0059	1.2591	1.5637
	ERR	0.0800	0.1333	0.1366	0.1379	0.1394	0.1405	0.1440	0.1529	0.1538	0.1619
	ACC	83.8095	84.6154	84.7059	85.6000	85.9459	86.0606	86.2069	86.3415	86.6667	92.0000
WRF	AUC	0.3212	0.0542	0.6768	0.1863	0.4380	0.1311	0.5405	0.3225	0.8430	0.9430
	ERR	0.1000	0.1200	0.1290	0.1429	0.1429	0.1440	0.1500	0.1538	0.1545	0.1684
	ACC	83.1579	84.5455	84.6154	85.0000	85.6000	85.7143	85.7143	87.0968	88.0000	90.0000

Table 6.4 shows the performance of various existing algorithms such as decision trees, gradient boosting and weighted random forest on random over sampling method. From the results of performance metric area under curve it is clear that weighted random forest performs better than the other algorithms. It is clear that in almost all iterations from 10 to 100, the performance AUC is better in gradient boosting method. This table also depicts the error performance of various existing algorithms such as decision trees, gradient boosting and weighted random forest on random over sampling method. From the results of performance metric error it is clear that gradient boosting reduces the error rate than the other algorithms such as decision tree and weighted random forest. Also, it is clear that in almost all iterations from 10 to 100, the performance error rate is reduced in gradient boosting method. The table shows the performance accuracy of the existing algorithms.

From all the iterations it can be understood that the gradient boosting algorithm performs better than that of other algorithms. Graphical representation of the comparison is given in Fig. 6.2.

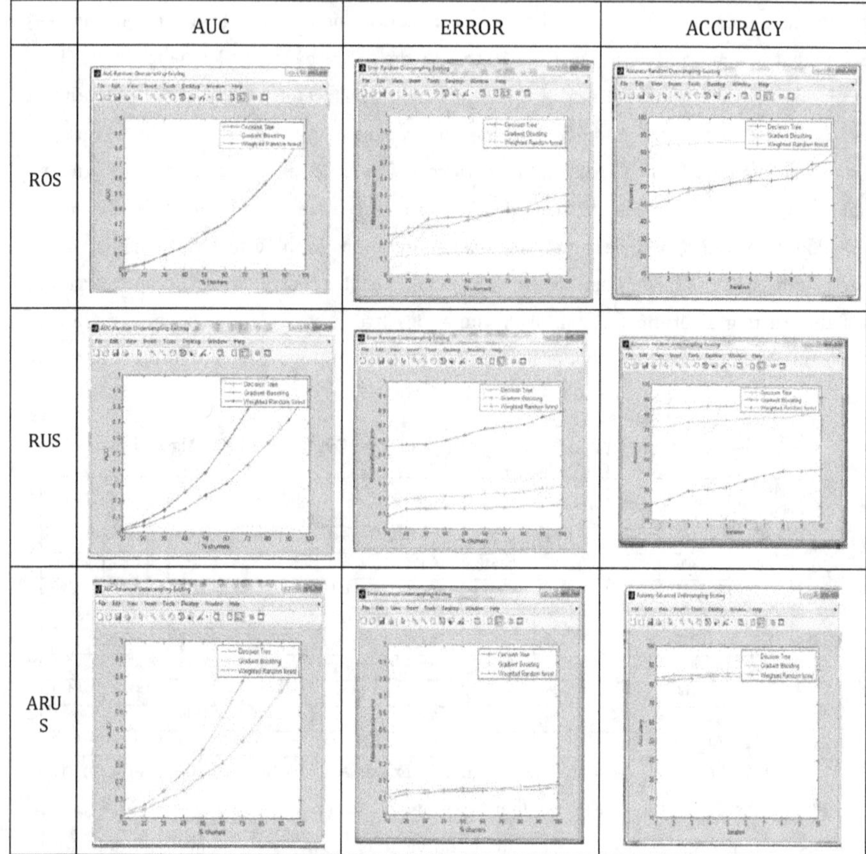

Figure 6.2: Comparison of DT, GB and WRF Algorithms in Different Sampling Method Using the AUC, Error and Accuracy

Genetic algorithm, a non-greedy technique, is proposed to handle imbalance classes. The technique makes use of candidate solution instead of single solution and then employs stochastic operators. It gives a conclusion that genetic algorithms work better with attribute interaction and thus avoids getting stuck into local maxima, which all together makes genetic algorithms suitable finding rarity. This would give a clear idea that for what reason genetic algorithms are being increasingly used for data mining. Several systems have relied on the power of genetic algorithms to handle rarity. Some of them used a genetic algorithm to predict very rare events while and other researchers tried to use a genetic algorithm to discover, small disjunct rules (Weiss, 2004).

Genetic algorithms imitate the process of evolution on an optimization problem. Each feasible solution of a problem is treated as an individual whose fitness is governed by the corresponding objective function value. A GA maintains a population of feasible solutions (also known as chromosomes) on which the concept of the survival of the fittest (among string structures) is applied. There is a structured yet randomized information exchange between two individuals (crossover operator) to give rise to better individuals. Diversity is added to the banking sectors by randomly changing some genes (mutation operator) or bringing in new individuals (immigration operator). A GA repeatedly applies these processes until the population converges. GAs can be implemented in a variety of ways. Several attempts have been taken to improve the performance of data mining systems with respect to rarity by choosing a more appropriate bias.

The simplest approach involves modifying existing systems to eliminate some small disjuncts based on tests of statistical significance or using error estimation techniques. The hope is that this will remove only improperly learned disjuncts (Weiss, 2001). Unfortunately, this approach was shown not only to degrade performance with respect to rarity, but also to degrade overall classification performance. This study, proposes the use of the decision tree algorithm, namely, C4.5. k-Nearest Neighbor is one of the most popular algorithms for text categorization. Many researchers have found that the k-NN algorithm achieves very good performance in their experiments on different data sets. The idea behind k-Nearest Neighbor algorithm is quite straightforward. To classify a new document, the system finds the k nearest neighbors among the training documents, and uses the categories of the k nearest neighbors to weight the category candidates. kNN algorithm is its efficiency, as it needs to compare a test document with all samples in the training set. In addition, the performance of this algorithm greatly depends on two factors, that is, a suitable similarity function and an appropriate value for the parameter.

When learning a set of classification rule for all classes, it is found that several rare classes are ignored and hence, the only solution is to predict rare classes. This technique is proven using Support vector machines and neural networks and one data mining technique that utilizes this recognition-based approach is a Hippo. Ripper is a rule induction system that utilizes a separate-and-conquer approach to iteratively build rules to cover previously uncovered training examples. Each rule is grown by adding conditions until no negative examples are covered. It normally generates rules for each class from the most 'rare class' to the most 'common class'.

Table 6.5: Random Over Sampling for GA, RA and k-NN Algorithms

Algorithm	Metrics	10	20	30	40	50	60	70	80	90	100
GA	AUC	0.7331	0.4315	0.3666	0.3594	0.2273	0.0295	0.1352	0.1785	0.5627	0.8204
	ERROR	0.1000	0.1440	0.1545	0.1548	0.1571	0.1579	0.1714	0.1750	0.2000	0.6308
	ACCU	36.9231	80.0000	82.5000	82.8571	84.2105	84.2857	84.5161	84.5455	85.6000	90.0000
RA	AUC	0.7632	0.05476	0.7500	0.3752	0.2863	0.2300	0.5295	0.4215	0.6000	0.8980
	ERR	0.1000	0.1440	0.1545	0.1548	0.1571	0.1579	0.1714	0.1875	0.2000	0.2000
	ACC	80.0000	80.0000	81.2500	82.8571	84.2105	84.2857	84.5161	84.5455	85.6000	90.0000
KNN	AUC	0.3222	0.0520	0.0670	0.4252	0.6613	0.7600	0.3425	0.7625	0.6432	0.7481
	ERR	0.1579	0.1600	0.1625	0.1677	0.1692	0.1786	0.1818	0.2000	0.2500	0.2857
	ACC	71.4286	75.0000	80.0000	81.8182	82.1429	83.0769	83.2258	83.7500	84.0000	84.2105

Table 6.5 shows the performance of various proposed algorithms such as genetic algorithm, ripper algorithm and k-nearest neighbor algorithm on random over sampling method. From the results of performance metric area under curve it is clear that genetic algorithm gives better performance than the ripper algorithm and k-nearest neighbor algorithm. It is clear that in almost all iterations from 10 to 100, the performance AUC is better in both genetic algorithm and k-nearest neighbor algorithm. This table also depicts the error performance of various proposed algorithms such as genetic algorithm, ripper algorithm and k-nearest neighbor algorithm. From the results of performance metric error it is clear that genetic algorithm and ripper algorithm reduces the error rate than the other algorithm namely k-nearest neighbor. Also, it is clear that in almost all iterations from 10 to 100, the performance error rate is reduced in genetic algorithm and ripper algorithm. The table shows the performance accuracy of the proposed algorithms. From all the iterations it can be understood that the genetic algorithm and ripper algorithm performs better than that of other algorithm. Graphical representation of the comparison is given in Fig. 6.3.

Table 6.6: Random Under Sampling for GA, RA and k-NN Algorithms

Algorithm	Metrics	10	20	30	40	50	60	70	80	90	100
GA	AUC	0.0068	0.0418	0.0744	0.1304	0.2079	0.3139	0.4248	0.5648	0.6962	0.8559
	ERROR	0.1440	0.1545	0.1548	0.1571	0.1579	0.1714	0.1875	0.2000	0.2000	0.7500
	ACCU	25.0000	80.0000	80.0010	81.2500	82.6571	84.2105	84.4357	84.5114	84.5321	85.6043
RA	AUC	0.0329	0.4171	0.0870	0.4241	0.3212	0.3862	0.8436	0.4203	0.1417	0.8743
	ERR	0.1000	0.1450	0.2345	0.1431	0.1471	0.2119	0.2014	0.2275	0.2130	0.2980
	ACC	81.0400	80.4400	81.2650	82.8565	84.2435	83.5557	84.4161	84.5675	85.6110	90.0110
KNN	AUC	0.2431	0.0450	0.9700	0.3252	0.3313	0.3540	0.4376	0.5025	0.6652	0.8544
	ERR	0.3219	0.1455	0.1067	0.1520	0.1438	0.1321	0.1870	0.2011	0.2430	0.2865
	ACC	71.4286	75.0000	80.0000	80.0000	81.2903	81.8182	83.0769	83.2000	83.7500	84.2105

Table 6.6 shows the performance of various proposed algorithms such as genetic algorithm, ripper algorithm and k-nearest neighbor algorithm on random under sampling method. From the results of performance metric area under curve it is clear that genetic algorithm is giving

better performance than the k-nearest neighbor algorithm and ripper algorithm. It is clear that in almost all iterations from 10 to 100, the performance AUC is better in genetic algorithm. This table also depicts the error performance of various proposed algorithms such as genetic algorithm, ripper algorithm and k-nearest neighbor algorithm. From the results of performance metric error it is clear that ripper algorithm reduces the error rate than the other algorithms namely k-nearest neighbor and genetic. Also, it is clear that in almost all iterations from 10 to 100, the performance error rate is reduced in ripper algorithm. The table shows the performance accuracy of the proposed algorithms. From all the iterations it can be understood that the ripper algorithm performs better than that of other two algorithms. Graphical representation of the comparison is given in Fig. 6.3.

Table 6.7: Advanced Random Under Sampling for GA, RA and k-NN Algorithms

Algorithm	Metrics	10	20	30	40	50	60	70	80	90	100
GA	AUC	0.0098	0.0353	0.0773	0.1287	0.2020	0.3166	0.4290	0.5724	0.6958	0.8516
	ERROR	0.1636	0.1750	0.1800	0.2000	0.2000	0.2065	0.2160	0.2786	0.3000	0.3429
	ACCU	65.7143	70.0000	72.1429	78.4000	79.3548	80.1000	80.0000	82.2100	82.5000	83.6364
RA	AUC	0.0114	0.0488	0.1061	0.1852	0.2690	0.3911	0.5402	0.6715	0.8408	1.0497
	ERR	0.0523	0.0532	0.0569	0.0600	0.0633	0.0642	0.0857	0.0870	0.1000	.2308
	ACC	76.9231	90.0000	91.3043	91.4286	93.5780	93.6709	94.0000	94.3089	94.6809	94.7712
KNN	AUC	0.0172	0.3450	0.0610	0.1242	0.2313	0.2200	0.3321	0.5224	0.6352	0.8861
	ERR	0.1560	0.1240	0.1563	0.1468	0.1779	0.1414	0.1744	0.2110	0.2300	0.2515
	ACC	73.7500	80.0000	80.0000	82.8571	82.8571	84.2105	84.5161	84.5455	85.6000	90.0000

Table 6.7 shows the performance of various proposed algorithms such as genetic algorithm, ripper algorithm and k-nearest neighbor algorithm on advanced random under sampling method. From the results of performance metric area under curve it is clear that genetic algorithm is giving better performance than the k-nearest neighbor algorithm and ripper algorithm. It is clear that in almost all iterations from 10 to 100, the performance AUC is better in genetic. This table also depicts the error performance of various proposed algorithms such as genetic algorithm, ripper algorithm and k-nearest neighbor algorithm.

From the results of performance metric error it is clear that ripper algorithm reduces the error rate than the other algorithms namely k-nearest neighbor and genetic. Also, it is clear that in almost all iterations from 10 to 100, the performance error rate is reduced in ripper algorithm.

The table shows the performance accuracy of the proposed algorithms. From all the iterations it can be understood that the k-nearest neighbor algorithm performs better than that of other two algorithms. Graphical representation of the comparison is given in Fig. 6.3.

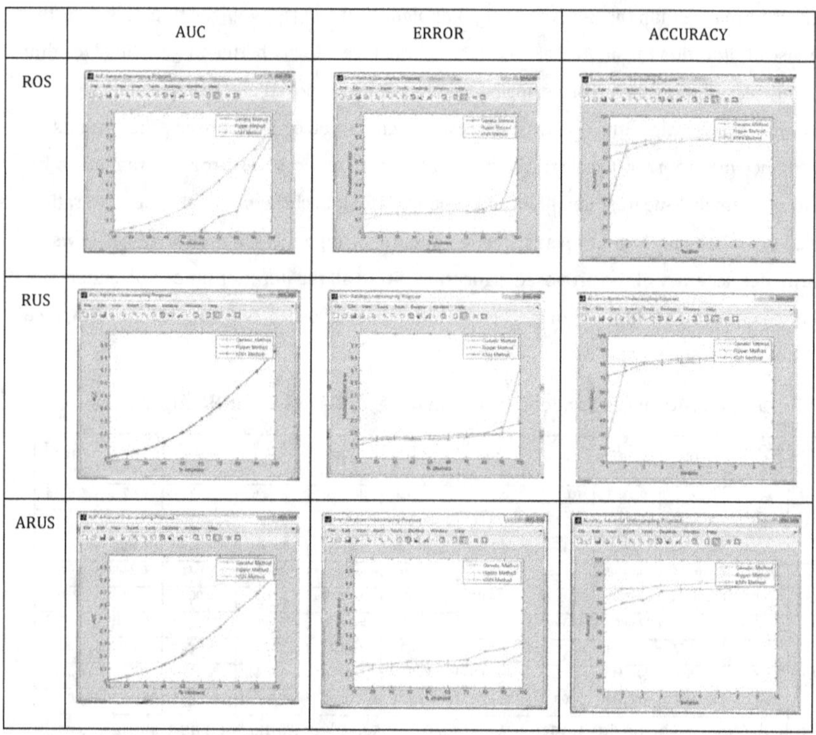

Figure 6.3: Comparison of GA, RA, k-NN algorithms in Different Sampling Method Using the AUC, Error and Accuracy

Table 6.8: Advanced Random Under Sampling for Ripper Algorithm and Modified Ripper Algorithm

Algorithm	Metrics	10	20	30	40	50	60	70	80	90	100
RA	AUC	0.0114	0.0488	0.1061	0.1852	0.2690	0.3911	0.5402	0.6715	0.8408	1.0497
	ERR	0.0523	0.0532	0.0569	0.0600	0.0633	0.0642	0.0857	0.0870	0.1000	.2308
	ACC	76.9231	90.0000	91.3043	91.4286	93.5780	93.6709	94.0000	94.3089	94.6809	94.7712
MRA	AUC	0.0151	0.0465	0.1070	0.1812	0.2716	0.3913	0.5408	0.6697	0.8410	1.0501
	ERR	0 .0459	0.0523	0.0532	0.0569	0.0580	0.0600	0.0615	0.0633	0.0857	0.1000
	ACC	90.0000	91.4286	93.6709	93.8462	94.0000	94.2029	94.3089	94.6809	94.7712	95.4128

Table 6.8 give one step more information about the comparison of ripper algorithm and modified ripper algorithm in terms of area under curve, error and accuracy during the different iterations in sampling methods which include advanced random under sampling method CUBE is used. Based on CUBE it is obtained that the inclusion probabilities from modified ripper algorithm iterations are accurately satisfied. Graphical representation of the

comparison between ripper algorithm and modified ripper algorithm is given in Fig. 6.4, 6.5, 6.6, 6.7.

	AUC	ERROR	ACCURACY
ARUS	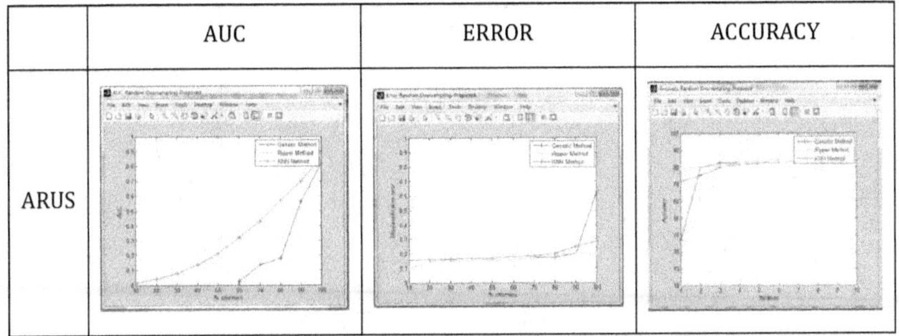		

Figure 6.4: Comparison of Ripper and Modified Ripper Algorithm with Advanced Random under Sampling

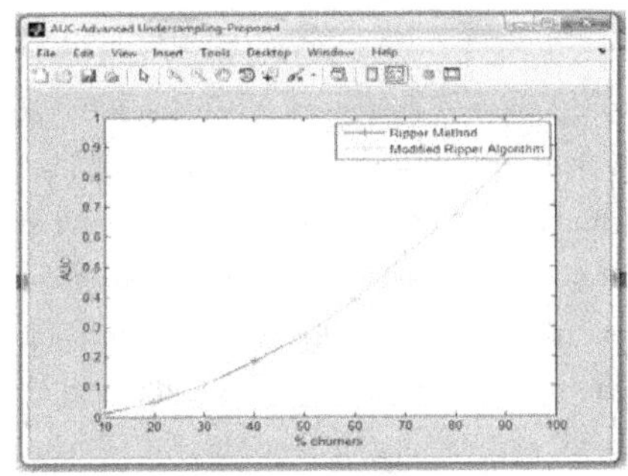

Figure 6.5: AUC and Advanced Under Sampling for RA and MRA

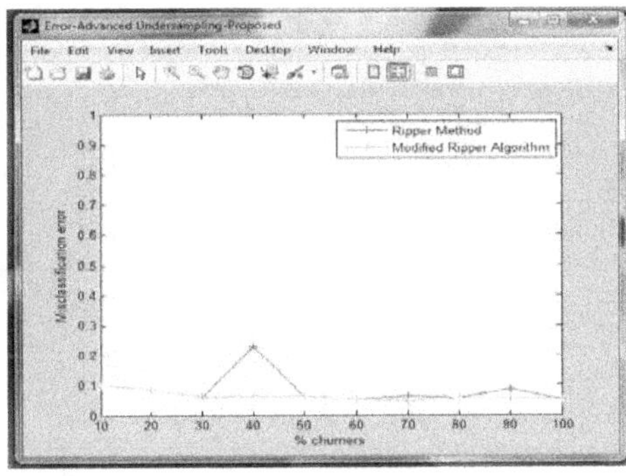

Figure 6.6: Misclassification Error and Advanced Under Sampling for RA and MRA

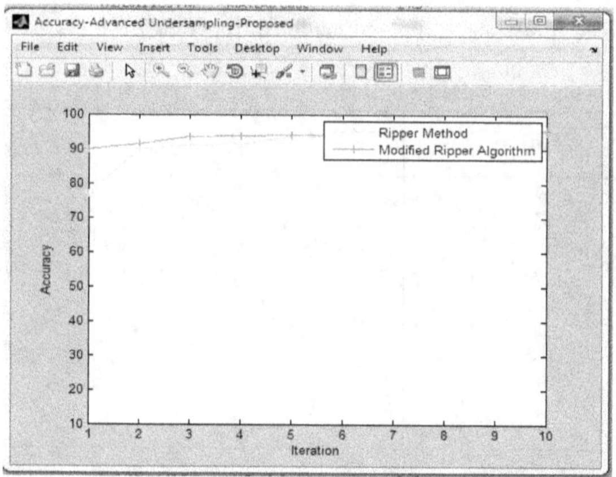

Figure 6.7: Accuracy and Advanced Under Sampling for RA and MRA

6.5.   Summary

The study thus predicts the churn of customers in banking sector and can then be extended, thereby helping formulate intervention strategies based on churn prediction to reduce the lost revenue by increasing customer retention. It is expected that, with a better understanding of these characteristics, bank managers can develop a customized approach to customer retention activities within the context of their Customer Relationship Management efforts. This chapter discussed the development of the Modified Ripper Algorithm and also introduced about the case study on banking sector and banking dataset towards customer churn prediction. The screenshots and results obtained out of the software prototype are tabulated and compared.

CHAPTER 7

RESULTS AND DISCUSSIONS

7.1. Introduction

This chapter summarises the results of this research. The performance metrics taken are Area Under Curve (AUC), error and accuracy. The algorithms such as decision tree, gradient boosting and weighted random forest are the existing algorithms discussed in literatures. Three sampling techniques namely Random Over Sampling, Random Under Sampling and Advanced Random Under Sampling along with seven algorithms (DT, GB, WRF, GA, RA, k-NN and MRA) are used for classification of churners. The Table 7.1 shows the performance of three algorithms.

Table 7.1: Performance of DRT, GB and WRF

SAMPLING METRICS	ROS			RUS			ARUS		
	DT	GB	WRF	DT	GB	WRF	DT	GB	WRF
AUC	0.34	0.35	0.35	0.55	0.61	0.35	0.6	0.61	0.35
Error	0.36	0.14	0.36	0.23	0.14	0.66	0.16	0.14	0.14
Accuracy	63.64	78.07	63.51	76.92	86.2	34.15	84.43	86.2	85.94

From the above results, several inferences have been made. In random over sampling, decision tree algorithm performs better with respect to AUC metric. In random under sampling and advanced random under sampling, weighted random forest provides better solution in terms of AUC. Error rate is considerably low while using gradient boosting algorithm in all sampling methods. Accuracy is better in gradient boosting algorithm in the said sampling methods. Overall it can be presumed that gradient boosting algorithm performs well than the decision tree and weighted random forest algorithms. Extensively three algorithms namely Genetic Algorithm, k-Nearest Neighbor Algorithm and Ripper Algorithm and Modified Ripper Algorithm are taken and applied to the churn prediction problem. From the literatures it is to be noted that the said three algorithms (GA, k-NN, RA and MRA) have not yet been applied in churn prediction. In this research these three algorithms are also applied for the churn prediction and the results are shown in Table 7.2.

Table 7.2: Performance Comparison of GA, k-NN, RA and MRA

SAMPLING \ METRICS		AUC	Error	Accuracy
ROS	GA	0.04	0.20	79.54
	k-NN	0.34	0.19	80.87
	RA	0.34	0.16	83.73
	MRA	0.04	0.06	93.94
RUS	GA	0.33	0.23	77.23
	k-NN	0.34	0.20	80.38
	RA	0.33	0.16	83.73
	MRA	0.29	0.05	95.50
ARUS	GA	0.33	0.23	77.37
	k-NN	0.34	0.17	82.83
	RA	0.33	0.16	83.54
	MRA	0.19	0.04	95.64

From the Table 7.2, it is shown that modified ripper algorithm is better that the genetic algorithm, k-nearest neighbor algorithm and ripper algorithm in terms of all the performance metrics AUC, error and accuracy with all sampling techniques random over sampling, random under sampling and advanced random under sampling. The modified ripper algorithm has performed less area under curve as 0.04, 0.29 and 0.19 in ROS, RUS and ARUS respectively. Also the proposed modified ripper algorithm has less error rate as 0.05, 0.05 and 0.04 in ROS, RUS and ARUS respectively. The accuracy performance is also better with modified ripper algorithm as 93.4, 95.5 and 95.64 percentage in ROS, RUS and ARUS. Overall it is presumed that the proposed modified ripper algorithm outperforms than the other algorithms in advanced random under sampling with respect to the churn prediction problem.

The class imbalance problem has been reported as a major obstacle to the induction of a good classifier. Oversampling and undersampling in data analysis are techniques used to adjust the class distribution of a data set (i.e. the ratio between the different classes/categories represented). Oversampling and under sampling are opposite and roughly equivalent techniques. They both involve using a bias to select more samples from one class than from another. The usual reason for oversampling is to correct for a bias in the original dataset. One scenario where it is useful is when training a classifier using labelled training data from a biased source, since labelled training data is valuable but often comes from unrepresentative sources. In this research the advanced random under sampling method is working better in analyzing the churners.

7.2.   Experiments and Results

Experiments were conducted to evaluate the performance of the proposed solutions to each data mining problem using a credit card holder dataset. The dataset consists of 1,00,000 records with 20 attributes. The attribute store data related to each customer. The attributes are Customer ID, Gender, Age, Tenure, Saving Amount, Current Amount, Time Deposits Amount, Funds Amount, Stocks Amount, Bank Assurance Amount, Life Assurance Amount, Business Loan Amount, Home Loan Amount, Consumer Loan Amount, Branch Transactions, ATM Transactions, Phone Transactions, Internet Transactions, Standing Orders and New Credit Card Flag. To compare classification algorithms, k-fold cross validation method has been used to estimate the accuracy of the algorithms. Table 7.1 presents the classification results of the three sampling methods, Random Over Sampling (ROS), Random Under Sampling (RUS) and Advanced Random Sampling (ARUS), when Decision Tree Regression (DTR), Gradient Boosting (GB) and Weighted Random Forest (WRF) are used. The results while using Genetic Algorithm (GA), k-Nearest Neighbor (k-NN), Ripper Algorithm (RA) and Modified Ripper Algorithm (MRA) for solving the data mining problem for addressing the class imbalance in customer churn prediction is shown in Table 7.2.

From the results, it can be seen that the churn prediction process has been improved by the proposed methods and is successful. Careful analysis further revealed that under-sampling leads to improved prediction accuracy. AUC and CUBE do not show any increase in predictive performance when compared with other under-sampling methods. Weighted random forests, as a cost-sensitive learner, perform significantly better. However, the performance of the Modified Ripper Algorithm has been better when compared to all other solutions. The modified ripper algorithm showed an efficiency gain of 10.87%, 12.32% and 12.65% on accuracy when compared with a ripper algorithm while using the ROS, RUS, ARUS sampling methods respectively.

Figure 7.1 shows the graphical representation of AUC, Error and Accuracy obtained by the three sampling techniques for the four classification methods GA, RM, k-NN and MRA respectively.

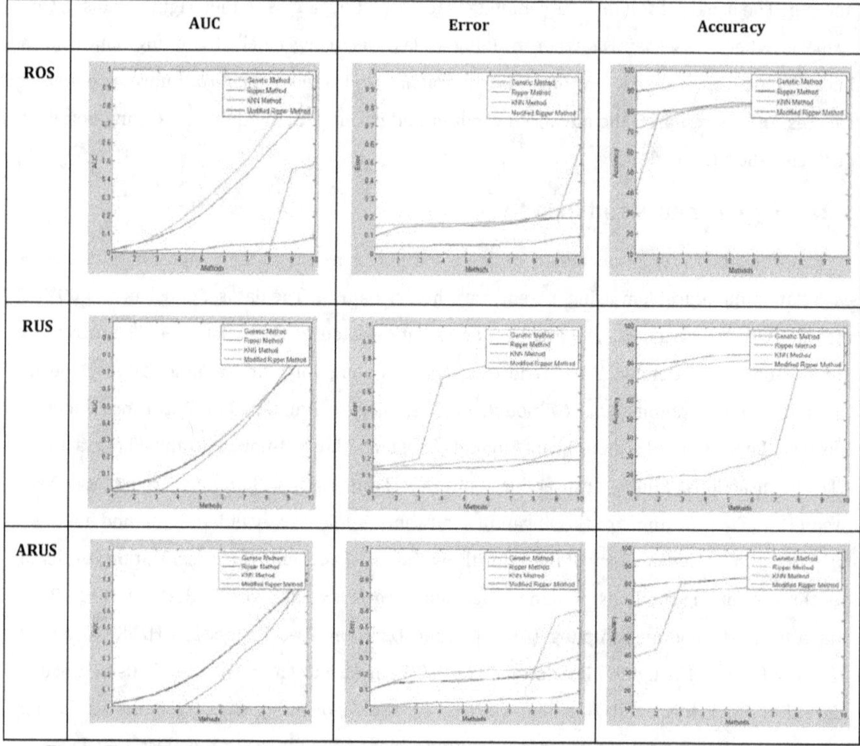

Figure 7.1: AUC, Error and Accuracy of Sampling Techniques and Classification Method

7.3. Summary

This chapter discussed the performance comparison of Decision Tree, Gradient Boosting, Weighted Random Forest, Genetic, k-Nearest Neighbour, Ripper Algorithm and Modified Ripper Algorithm by using the performance metric namely area under curve, error and accuracy. Finally, it shows that the proposed algorithm namely "Modified Ripper Algorithm" has high performance in predicting the churners in bank under the domain credit-card holders i.e., Modified Ripper Algorithm is working better in analyzing the churners.

CHAPTER 8

CONCLUSIONS AND FURTHER RESEARCH

8.1. Conclusions

Customer Relationship Management (CRM) application aids in taking care of the current and future customers. Using effective and efficient CRM sales, marketing, and customer service teams, interactions with customers are all managed in one place. Having accurate and up-to-date customer information will help in making better business decisions. Customer churn is the thrust terminology in the banking sector. It tries to denote the movement of customers from one bank to another. In particular, the banking industry, identifying probable churn customers has increased in its importance in the recent past. In domain of banking, it is defined a churn customer as one who closes all his/her accounts and stops doing business with the bank. Customer preservation also known as customer retention is an increasingly great issue in today's ever competitive commercial and banking area. Additional competition and increased regulation made it more difficult for banks to stand out from the crowd.

Studies carried out at international and national levels indicate the significance of a few imperatives for commercial banks for their survival and growth such as customer retention, focussing on technology, specific market segments, enhanced productivity and efficiency. Customer retention is first and foremost method for the growth of the banks. Customer Relationship Management tools have been developed and applied in order to improve customer acquisition and retention and to support important analytical tasks such as predictive modelling and classification. In real time, the bank does not always capture feedback data. Customer churn is one of the top issues for most banks. It costs significantly more to obtain new customers than keep hold of existing ones and it costs far more to reacquire redirected customers. In reality, quite a few empirical studies and models have proven that churn remains one of the biggest destructors of enterprise importance.

8.2. Achievements

Churn is often a rare object, but of great interest and great value class imbalance has not received much attention in the context of data mining. This research investigates the methods for handling class imbalance in churn prediction in a better way. To investigate the impact of these methods, banking customer churn prediction data set is used. Sampling (Random Under, Random Over and Advanced Under-Sampling), Decision Tree, Boosting (Gradient Boosting

Machine), Cost Sensitive Learner (Weighted Random Forests), Non Greedy Search Technique (Genetic Algorithm), Using a More Appropriate Inductive Bias (k-NN Algorithm), Learn Only The Rare Classes (Ripper Algorithm) are implemented. More Appropriate Evaluation Metrics (AUC, Error and Accuracy) are compared. Results show that under-sampling can lead to improved prediction accuracy, especially when evaluated with AUC. It is found that there is no need to under-sample so that there are as many churners in your training set as non churners. The advanced sampling technique CUBE increased predictive performance.

In this research work, in order to obtain an extra edge over competitive business, banking sector is relying more and more on CRM combined with datamining techniques. The churning behaviour of credit card holders is predicted in the presence of class imbalance. Presence of imbalance during churn process reduces the efficiency of prediction and therefore has to be handled carefully. Five types of rare case categories were identified and nine types of predictors were proposed to handle class imbalance in credit card holder churning prediction. Four types of sampling methods were also analyzed. Experimental results showed that all the proposed methods are successful for churn prediction upon which the Modified Ripper Algorithm outperforms all the other algorithms.

8.3. Limitations

This research work on design and development of customer churn prediction through class imbalance using new algorithm improves both the efficiency and effectiveness of predicting churn. The limitations of this research are:

- This research is restricted to Genetic algorithm, k-Nearest Neighbour, Ripper and Modified Ripper algorithms and not for some state of the art techniques such as Support Vector Machine, Bayesian methods and Neural Networks.
- For comparing AUCs over two or more algorithms on a data set, doing k fold cv or 5x2 cv, a test statistic should be developed to test significant difference is not calculated.

8.4. Recommendations for Further Research

The research work is concerned with the study of customer churn prediction and class imbalance, study and analysis of existing algorithms for churn prediction, development of new algorithm which improves efficiency and effectiveness of prediction. This can be further extended in the following directions:

- Direction towards assessing the usefulness of sampling in logistic regression in order to compare the differences in performance of alternative predictive models.

- Nowadays, there is no complete working meta-theory to assist with selection of the correct kernel function and SVM parameters. Deriving a procedure to select the proper kernel function and correct parameter values according to the specific type of classification problem is an interesting topic for further research.

- Furthermore, applying SVMs using sufficient sample size can be very time consuming due to the long computational time and often requires specific software. In order to adopt SVMs in related work is user friendly and need to be incorporated into traditional data mining software tools.

BIBLIOGRAPHY

1. M. Abdous and C.J. Yen, "A predictive study of learner satisfaction and outcomes in face-to-face, satellite broadcast, and live video-streaming learning environments", The Internet and Higher Education, Vol.13, Pp.248-257, 2010.

2. S.R. Ahmed, "Applications of data mining in retail business", Proceedings International Conference in Information Technology: Coding and Computing (ITCC), Vol.2, Pp.455-459, 2004.

3. J. Ahn, S. Han and Y. Lee, "Customer churn analysis: Churn determinants and mediation effects of partial defection in the Korean mobile telecommunications service industry", Telecom. Policy, Vol.30, Pp.552-568, 2006.

4. R. Alejo, J.M. Sotoca, R.M. Valdovinos and G.A. Casan, "The multiclass imbalance problem: Cost functions with modular and non-modular neural networks", Proc. 6th Int. Symp. Neural Netw., Vol.56, Pp.421–431, 2009.

5. Ansari and Mela, "E-Customization", Journal of marketing research, Vol.40, No.2, Pp.131-145, 2003.

6. N. Arora, X. Dreze, A. Ghose, J.D. Hess, R. Iyengar, B. Jing, Y. Joshi, V. Kumar, N. Lurie, S. Neslin and S. Sajeesh, "Putting one-to-one marketing to work: Personalization, customization, and choice", Marketing Letters, Vol.19, No.3-4, Pp.305-321, 2008.

7. P. Ataee, "Mining the (data) bank", IEEE Potentials, Vol.24, No.4, Pp. 40-42, 2005.

8. W.H. Au, K.C.C. Chan and X. Yao, "A novel evolutionary data mining algorithm with applications to churn prediction", IEEE Transactions on Evolutionary Computation, Vol.7, Pp.532-545, 2003.

9. B. Baesens, S. Viaene, D. Van Den Poel, J. Vanthienen and G. Dedene, "Bayesian Neural Network Learning for Repeat Purchase Modelling in Direct Marketing", European Journal of Operational Research, Vol.138, No.1, Pp.191-211, 2002.

10. R. Barandela, R.M. Valdovinos, J.S. Sanchez and F.J. Ferri, "The imbalanced training sample problem: Under or over sampling?", Proc. Joint IAPR Int. Workshops SSPR/SPR, Vol.3138, Pp. 806–814, 2004.

11. A.P. Bradley, "The use of the area under the roc curve in the evaluation of machine learning algorithms", Pattern Recognit., Vol.30, No.7, Pp.1145–1159, 1997.

12. L. Breiman, J. Friedman, R. Olshen and C. Stone, "Classification and Regression Trees", Wadsworth Int. Group, 1984.

13. G. Brown, J.L. Wyatt and P. Tino, "Managing diversity in regression ensembles", J. Mach. Learn. Res., Vol.6, Pp.1621–1650, 2005.

14. W. Buckinx, E. Moons, D.V.D. Poel and G. Wets, "Customer-adapted coupon targeting using feature selection", Expert Systems with Applications, Vol.26, Pp.509-518, 2004.

15. J. Burez and D. Van Den Poel, "Handling class imbalance in customer churn prediction", Expert Syst. Appl., Vol.36, Pp.4626-4636, 2009.

16. N.V. Chawla, K.W. Bowyer, L.O. Hall and W.P. Kegelmeyer, "Smote: Synthetic minority over-sampling technique", J. Artif. Intell. Res., Vol.16, No.1, Pp.321–357, 2002.

17. N.V. Chawla, A. Lazarevic, L.O. Hall and K. Bowyer, "SMOTEBoost: Improving prediction of the minority class in boosting", Proc. Principles Knowl. Discov. Databases, Pp. 107–119, 2003.

18. C. Chen, A. Liaw and L. Breiman, "Using random forest to learn imbalanced data", University of California, Berkeley, Vol.110, Pp.1-12, 2004.

19. Y.L. Chen, C.L. Hsu and S.C. Chou, "Constructing a multi-valued and multilabeled decision tree", Expert Systems with Applications, Vol.25, Pp.199-209, 2003.

20. C. Chui, B. Kao and E. Hung, "Mining frequent itemsets from uncertain data", Proceeding of the Methodologies for Knowledge Discovery and Data Mining, Pacific-Asia Conference (PAKDD), 2007.

21. K. Cios, A. Teresinska, S. Konieczna, J. Potocka and S. Sharma, "Diagnosing myocardial perfusion from SPECT bull's-eye maps–a knowledge discovery approach", IEEE Engineering in Medicine and Biology Magazine, special issue on Medical Data Mining and Knowledge Discovery, Vol.19, No.4, Pp.17–25, 2000.

22. R. Collobert, S. Bengio and J. Marithoz, "Torch: A Modular Machine Learning Software Library", Technical Report IDIAP-RR 02-46, IDIAP 2002.

23. K. Coussement and D. Van Den Poel, "Churn Prediction in Subscription Services: An Application of Support Vector Machines While Comparing Two Parameter-Selection Techniques", Forthcoming in Expert Systems with Applications, 2008.

24. D. Ruan, G. Chen, E.E. Kerre and G. Wets, eds. "Intelligent data mining: techniques and applications", Springer Science & Business Media, 2005.

25. David Hand, Heikki Mannila and Padhraic Smyth, "Principles of Data Mining", The MIT Press, 2001.

26. D.V. Den Poel and B. Lariviere, "Customer attrition analysis for financial services using proportional hazard models", European Journal of Operational Research, Vol.157, No.1, Pp.196-217, 2004.

27. P. Domingos, "The role of occam's razor in knowledge discovery", Data Min. Knowl. Discov., Vol.3, No.4, Pp.409-425, 1999.

28. J.H. Drew, D.R. Mani, A.L. Betz and P. Datta, "Targeting customers with statistical and Data-Mining techniques", Journal of Service Research, Vol.3, No.3, Pp.205-219, 2001.

29. C. Elkan, "The foundations of cost-sensitive learning", Proc. 17th Int. Conf. Mach. Learn, Pp.239–246, 2001.

30. A. Estabrooks, T. Jo and N. Japkowicz, "A multiple resampling method for learning from imbalanced data sets", Comput. Intell., Vol.20, No.1, Pp.18–36, 2004.

31. W. Fan, S.J. Stolfo, J. Zhang and P.K. Chan, "AdaCost:Misclassification cost-sensitive boosting", Proc. 16th Int. Conf. Mach. Learn., Pp.97–105, 1999.

32. U. Fayyad, G. Piatesky-Shapiro, P. Smyth and R. Uthurusamy (Eds.), "Advances in Knowledge Discovery and Data Mining", AAAI Press, Cambridge, 1996.

33. A. Fernandez, M.J. Del Jesus and F. Herrera, "Multi-class imbalanced data-sets with linguistic fuzzy rule based classification systems based on pairwise learning", Comput. Intell. Knowledge Based Syst. Des., Vol.6178, Pp.89–98, 2010.

34. J. Ferreira, M. Vellasco, M. Pachecco and C. Barbosa, "Data mining techniques on the evaluation of wireless churn", Proceedings–European Symposium on Artificial Neural Networks Bruges, 2004.

35. Francis Buttle, "Customer Relationship Management: Concepts and Technologies", 2nd Edition, 2008.

36. Freund and Schapire, "A decision-theoretic generalization of on-line learning and an application to boosting", Journal of Computer and System Sciences, Vol.55, No.1, Pp.119–139, 1997.

37. Y. Freund and R. Schapire, "Experiments with a new boosting algorithm", Proc. 13th Int. Conf. Mach. Learn., Pp.148–156, 1996.

38. S. Garcia, J. Derrac, I. Triguero, J. Carmonac and F. Herrera, "Evolutionary-based selection of generalized instances for imbalanced classification", Knowl.-Based Syst., Vol.25, No.1, Pp.3–12, 2012.

39. S. Garcia, N. Pedrajas, J.A. Romero Del Castillo and D. Ortiz-Boyer, "A cooperative coevolutionary algorithm for instance selection for instance based learning", Mach. Learn., Vol.78, No.3, Pp.381–420, 2010.

40. C. Giraud-Carrier and O. Povel, "Characterising data mining software", Intell. Data Anal, Vol.7, No.3, Pp.181-192, 2003.

41. S. Graves, D. Kletter, W. Hetzel and R. Bolton, "A dynamic model of the duration of the customer's relationship with a continuous service provider: The role of satisfaction", Market. Sci., Vol.17, No.1, Pp.45-65, 1998.

42. H. Guo and H.L. Viktor, "Learning from imbalanced data sets with boosting and data generation: The DataBoost-IM approach", ACM SIGKDD Explor. Newslett., Vol.6, No.1, Pp.30–39, 2004.

43. J. Hadden, A. Tiwari, R. Roy and D. Ruta, "Computer assisted customer churn management: State-of-the-art and future trends", Computers & Operations Research, Vol.34, No.10, Pp.2902-2917, 2007.

44. J. Hadden, A. Tiwari, R. Roy and D. Ruta, "Churn prediction using complaints data", International Journal of Intelligent Technology, Vol.13, Pp.158-163, 2006.

45. H. Han, W.Y. Wang and B.H. Mao, "Borderline-SMOTE: A new over-sampling method in imbalanced data sets learning", Proc. ICIC, Lecture Notes in Computer Science, New York, Pp.878–887, 2005.

46. T.R. Hancock, T. Jiang, M. Li and P.J. Trom, "Lower Bounds on Learning Decision Lists and Trees", Information and Computation, Vol.126, No.2, Pp.114-122, 1996.

47. D.J. Hand and R.J. Till, "A simple generalisation of the area under the roc curve for multiple class classification problems", Mach. Learn., Vol.45, No.2, Pp.171–186, 2001.

48. T. Hastie and R. Tibshirani, "Classification by pairwise coupling", Ann. Statist, Vol.26, No.2, Pp.451–471, 1998.

49. H. He and E.A. Garcia, "Learning from imbalanced data", IEEE Trans. Knowl. Data Eng., Vol.21, No.9, Pp.1263–1284, 2009.

50. T.K. Ho, "Random Decision Forest", Proceedings of the 3rd International Conference on Document Analysis and Recognition, Pp.278–282, 1995.

51. J. Hoekstra and E. Huizingh, "The Lifetime Value Concept in Customer Based Marketing", Journal of Market Focused Management, Vol.3, Pp.257-274, 1999.

52. K. Hot, J.J. Hull and S.N. Srihari, "Decision combination in multiple classifier systems," IEEE Trans. Pattern Anal. Mach. Intell., Vol.16, No.1, Pp.66–75, 1994.

53. S.Y. Hung, D.C. Yen and H.Y. Wang, "Applying data mining to telecom churn management", Expert Systems with Applications, Vol.31, Pp.515-524, 2006.

54. H. Hwang, T. Jung and E. Suh, "An LTV model and customer segmentation based on customer value: a case study on the wireless telecommunication industry", Expert Systems with Applications, Vol.26, No.2, Pp.181-188, 2004.

55. L. Hyafl and R.L. Rivest, "Constructing optimal binary decision trees is NP complete", Information Processing Letters, Vol.5, No.1, Pp.15-17, 1976.

56. Ian H. Witten and Eibe Frank, "Data Mining Practical Machine Learning Tools and Techniques", Second edition, Elsevier, 2005.

57. T. Iwata, K. Saito and T. Yamada, "Recommendation method for extending subscription periods", Proceedings of the 12th ACM SIGKDD international conference on Knowledge discovery and data mining, Pp.574-579, 2006.

58. C.Z. Janikow, "A knowledge-intensive genetic algorithm for supervised learning", Mach. Learn., Vol.13, Pp.189–228, 1993.

59. F. Japkowicz, "Learning from imbalanced data sets: A comparison of various strategies", Proc. AAAI Workshop Learn. From Imbalanced Data Sets, Pp.10–15, 2000.

60. N. Japkowicz, C. Myers and M.A. Gluck, "A novelty detection approach to classification", Proc. IJCAI, Pp.518–523, 1995.

61. J.R. Jiao, Y. Zhang and M. Helander, "A Kansei Mining system for affective design", Expert Systems with Applications, Vol.30, Pp.658-673, 2006.

62. Jiawei Han and Micheline Kamber, "Data Mining: Concepts and Techniques", Second Edition, 2006.

63. M.V. Joshi, V. Kumar and R.C. Agarwal, "Evaluating boosting algorithms to classify rare classes: Comparison and improvements", Proc. IEEE Int. Conf. Data Mining, Pp.257–264, 2001.

64. S. Keaveney and M. Parthasarathy, "Customer switching behaviour in online services: An exploratory study of the role of selected attitudinal, behavioural, and demographic factors", J. ACAD. Market. Sci., Vol.29, No.4, Pp.374-390, 2001.

65. T.M. Khoshgoftaar, C. Seiffert, J. Van Hulse, A. Napolitano and A. Folleco, "Learning with limited minority class data", Proc. 6th ICMLA, Pp.348–353, 2007.

66. Y.S. Kim and W.N. Street, "An intelligent system for customer targeting: A data mining approach", Decision Support Systems, Vol.37, Pp.215-228, 2004.

67. E.M. Kleinberg, "An overtraining-resistant stochastic modeling method for pattern recognition", The annals of statistics, Vol.24, No.6, Pp.2319-2349, 1996.

68. M. Kubat, R. Holte and S. Matwin, "Learning when negative examples abound", Proc. 9th Eur. Conf. Mach. Learn., Vol.1224, Pp.146–153, 1997.

69. M. Kubat and S. Matwin, "Addressing the curse of imbalanced training sets: One-sided selection", Proc. 14th Int. Conf. Mach. Learn., Pp.179–186, 1997.

70. A. Kumar, "From mass customization to mass personalization: a strategic transformation", International Journal of Flexible Manufacturing Systems, Vol.19, No.4, Pp.533-547, 2007.

71. O. Gervasi, M.L. Gavrilova, V. Kumar, A. Laganà, H.P. Lee, Y. Mun, D. Taniar and C.J.K. Tan (Eds.), "Computational Science and Its Applications ICCSA", Vol.3, Pp.181-189, 2005.

72. B. Larivière and D. Van den Poel, "Investigating the role of product features in preventing customer churn, by using survival analysis and choice modeling: The case of financial services", Expert Systems with Applications, Vol.27, No.2, Pp.277-285, 2004.

73. D.T. Larose, "Discovering Knowledge in Data: An Introduction to Data Mining", John Wiley & Sons, Inc, 2005.

74. G. Linden, B. Smith and J. York, "Amazon.com recommendations: Item-to-item collaborative filtering", IEEE Internet computing, Vol.7, No.1, Pp.76-80, 2003.

75. Ling Xie, Dan Li and Jin Xiao, "Feature selection based transfer ensemble model for customer churn prediction", International Conference on System Science, Engineering Design and Manufacturing Informatization, Vol.2, Pp.134-137, 2011.

76. C. Ling and G. Li, "Data mining for direct marketing problems and solutions", Proc. 4th Int. Conf. KDD, New York, Pp.73–79, 1998.

77. D. Liu and Y. Shih, "Integrating AHP and data mining for product recommendation based on customer lifetime value", Information & Management, Vol.42, No.3, Pp.387-400, 2005.

78. D. Mease, A.J. Wyner and A. Buja, "Boosted classification trees and class probability/ quantile estimation", J. MACH. Learn. Res., Vol.8, Pp.409–439, 2007.

79. T. Mitchell, "Machine Learning", WCB/Mc Graw Hill, 1997.

80. Mobasher, Berendt and Spiliopoulou, "Knowledge Discovery and Data for Personalization", Tutorial at the 12th European Conference on Machine Learning, Freiburg, 2001.

81. Mobasher, Cooley and Srivastava, "Automatic Personalization Based on Web Usage Mining", Communications of the Association for Computing Machinery, Vol.43, No.8, Pp.142-151, 2000.

82. M.C. Mozer, R. Wolniewicz, D.B. Grimes, E. Johnson and H. Kaushansky, "Predicting subscriber dissatisfaction and improving retention in the wireless telecommunications industry", IEEE Transactions on Neural Networks, Vol.11, Pp.690-696, 2000.

83. S. Mukherjea, B. Bamba and P. Kankar, "Information retrieval and knowledge discovery utilizing a biomedical patent semantic Web", IEEE Transactions on Knowledge and Data Engineering, Vol.17, No.8, Pp.1099–1110, 2005.

84. A. Nairn, "CRM: helpful or full of hype?", The Journal of Database Marketing, Vol.9, No.4, Pp.376-382, 2002.

85. G.E. Naumov, "NP-completeness of problems of construction of optimal decision trees", Soviet Physics: Doklady, Vol.36, No.4, Pp.270-271, 1991.

86. E. Ngai, "Customer relationship management research (1992-2002): An academic literature review and classification", Marketing Intelligence & Planning, Vol.23, No.6, Pp.582-605, 2005.

87. E.W.T. Ngai, L. Xiu and D.C.K. Chau, "Application of data mining techniques in customer relationship management: A literature relationship and classification", Expert Systems with Applications, Vol.36, 2009.

88. Omkar Singh Lodhi, "Most Commonly Used Techniques In Data Mining", International Journal of Advances in Engineering Research, Vol.4, No.III, 2012.

89. Pancras and Sudhir, "Optimal Marketing Strategies for a Customer Data Intermediary", Journal of Marketing Research, Vol.44, No.4, Pp.560-578, 2007.

90. A. Parvatiyar and J.N. Sheth, "Customer relationship management: emerging practice, process and discipline", Journal of Economic and Social Research, Vol.3, Pp.6-23, 2002.

91. U.D. Prasad and S. Madhavi, "Prediction of churn behavior of bank customers using data mining tools", Business Intelligence Journal, Vol.5, Pp.96-101, 2012.

92. A. Prinzie and D. Van Den Poel, "Incorporating sequential information into traditional classification models by using an element/position sensitive SAM", Decision Support Systems, Vol.42, No.2, Pp.508-526, 2006.

93. A. Prinzie and D. Van Den Poel, "Random Forests for Multiclass classification: Random Multinomial Logit", Expert Systems with Applications, Vol.35, No.3, 2008.

94. J.R. Quinlan, "Simplifying decision trees", International Journal of Man Machine Studies, Vol.27, Pp.221-234, 1987.

95. J.R. Quinlan, "C4.5: programs for machine learning", Morgan Kaufmann, Publishers Inc., San Francisco, CA, USA, 1993.

96. Reinartz and Venkatesan, "Decision Models for Customer Relationship Management", Handbook of Marketing Decision Models, Springer Netherlands, Dordrecht, 2009.

97. R. Rifkin and A. Klautau, "In defense of one-vs-all classification", J. Mach. Learn. Res., Vol.5, Pp.101–141, 2004.

98. C.V. Rijsbergen, Information Retrieval. London, U.K.: Butterworths, 1979.

99. L. Rokach, "Ensemble-based classifier", Artif. Intell. Rev., Vol.33, No.1–2, Pp.1–39, 2010.

100. S. Rosset, E. Neumann, U. Eick, N. Vatnik and Y. Idan, "Customer lifetime value modeling and its use for customer retention planning", KDD Proceedings of the Eighth ACM SIGKDD International Conference on Knowledge Discovery and Data Mining, Pp.332-340, 2002.

101. R. Rust, A. Zahorik and T. Keiningham, "Return on quality (ROQ): Making service quality financially accountable", J. Market., Vol.59, Pp.58-70, 1995.

102. C. Seiffert, T.M. Khoshgoftaar, J. Van Hulse and A. Napolitano, "Building useful models from imbalanced data with sampling and boosting", Proc. 21st Int. FLAIRS Conf., Pp.306–311, 2008.

103. C. Shearer, "The CRISP-DM model: the new blueprint for data mining", Journal of Data Warehousing, Vol.5, No.4, Pp.13–19, 2000.

104. Subhasish Das, "Customer Relationship Management", Excel Books, 2007

105. Y. Sun, M.S. Kamel and Y. Wang, "Boosting for learning multiple classes with imbalanced class distribution", Proc. 6th ICDM, Pp.592–602, 2006.

106. Y. Sun, M.S. Kamel, A.K.C. Wong and Y. Wang, "Cost-sensitive boosting for classification of imbalanced data", Pattern Recognit., Vol.40, No.12, Pp.3358–3378, 2007.

107. Y. Sun, A.K. Wong and Y. Wang, "Parameter inference of cost-sensitive boosting algorithms", Proc. 4th Int. Conf. Mach. Learn. Data Mining Pattern Recognit, Pp.21–30, 2005.

108. Surjeet Kumar Yadav, Brijeshbharadwaj and Saurabh Pal, "A comparative Study for Predicting Student's performance", International Journal of Innovative technology and creative engineering, Vol.1, No.12, 2011.

109. K. Tang, P.N. Suganthan and X. Yao, "An analysis of diversity measures", Mach. Learn., Vol.65, Pp.247–271, 2006.

110. T.S.H. Teo, P. Devadoss and S.L. Pan, "Towards a holistic perspective of customer relationship management implementation: A case study of the housing and development board", Decision Support Systems, Vol.42, Pp.1613-1627, 2006.

111. K.M. Ting, "A comparative study of cost-sensitive boosting algorithms", Proc. 17th Int. Conf. Mach. Learn., Pp.983–990, 2000.

112. E. Turban, J.E. Aronson, T.P. Liang and R. Sharda, "Decision support and business intelligence systems", (Eighth ed.)., Pearson Education, 2007.

113. Tuzhilin and Adomavicius, "Export-Driven Validation of Rule-Based User Models in Personalization Applications", Data Mining and Knowledge Discovery, Vol.5, Pp.33-58, 2001.

114. A. Ultsch, "Data mining and knowledge discovery with emergent self-organizing feature maps for multivariate time series", E. Oja and S. Kaski, editors, Kohonen Maps, Elsevier, Pp.33-45, 1999.

115. J. Van Hulse, T.M. Khoshgoftaar and A. Napolitano, "Experimental perspectives on learning from imbalanced data", Proc. 24th Int. Conf. Mach. Learn., Corvallis, Pp.935–942, 2007.

116. S. Viaene, B. Baesens, T. Van Gestel, J.A.K. Suykens, D. Van Den Poel, J. Vanthienen, B. De Moor and G. Dedene, "Knowledge Discovery in a direct marketing case using least squares support vector machines", International Journal of Intelligent Systems, Vol.16, No.9, 2001.

117. Wang and Jiang, "Mining Actionable Patterns by Role Models", IEEE International Conference on Data Engineering, Atlanta, Pp.16-25, 2006.

118. S. Wang and X. Yao, "Negative Correlation Learning for Class Imbalance Problems", School of Computer Science, University of Birmingham, 2012.

119. G.M. Weiss, "Mining with rarity: A unifying framework", ACM SIGKDD Explor. Newslett., Vol.6, No.1, Pp.7–19, 2004.

120. G.M. Weiss and F. Provost, "Learning when training data are costly: The effect of class distribution on tree induction", J. Artif. Intell. Res., Vol.19, Pp.315–354, 2003.

121. G.M. Weiss and F. Provost, "The effect of class distribution on classifier learning: An empirical study", Dept. Comput. Sci., Rutgers Univ., Newark, NJ, Tech. Rep. TR-43, 2001.

122. Y. Yang and B. Padmanabhan, "A hierarchical pattern-based clustering algorithm for grouping web transactions", IEEE Transaction on Knowledge and Data Engineering Vol.17, Pp.1300-1304, 2005.

123. H. Zantema and H.L. Bodlaender, "Finding Small Equivalent Decision Trees is Hard", International Journal of Foundations of Computer Science, Vol.11, No.2, Pp.343-354, 2000.

124. Zhang and Wedel, "The Effectiveness of Customized Promotions in Online and Offline Store", Journal of Marketing Research, Vol.46, No.2, Pp.190-206, 2009.

125. Z.H. Zhou and X.Y. Liu, "Training cost-sensitive neural networks with methods addressing the class imbalance problem", IEEE Trans. Knowledge, Data Eng., Vol.18, No.1, Pp.63–77, 2006.